Bobby Brown

The Truth, the Whole Truth and Nothing But . . .

Contributors

Liwaza Green; Robert and Sandra Smith; Sun-raOOWWEE Shakur; Yusef Hoard; Jason King; Tommy Brown; Carolyn Brown; Carole Brown; Kelsey Brown; Shane Brown; Solomon Smallwood; Emerson Carey Jr.; Ifetayo Green; The Britto Agency—Marvet Britto and Rachel; BookMasters, Inc.—Shelly Sapyta, Tim Snider, Kim Wertman, and the entire BookMasters staff; Nico at Nico Designs; Topkat; Joseph Lovett, Paula Froelich, Rodger Friedman, Karu Daniels, Lee Bailey, Natasha Daniels, Gina Fusco, and Charles Fisher.

Foreword

By author Derrick Handspike

The birth of this book started off as an autobiography about Bobby's life that was to be co-written by me and Bobby. The book was set to be published under my company Down South Books and Bobby and I were going to reap the benefits. Somewhere between the completion of the book and the media blitz that occurred from the controversial quotes from the manuscript that were leaked to the New York Post, it seemed as though Bobby got cold feet and started to procrastinate on our final agreement and the promotional and marketing planning phase of the project. Among other things, there were a few quotes leaked about his marriage to Whitney Houston and how he started the downward spiral of drug abuse that turned him into the Bobby we hear about in the tabloids. Undeniably, the quotes were blown out of proportion and made headlines all over the world. This book had just about as much coverage as the infamous O.J. Simpson trial that swept the nation years prior. It got more coverage than all the newsworthy moments of that time such as the Jay Z and Beyonce' wedding, Michael Jackson's 25th year Thriller Anniversary, and more coverage than the Presidential election. How does a book on someone's life get more press than the aforementioned news? Of course, it has to be drama or something very negative. Whatever the reason, I think this left a bad taste in Bobby's mouth about going forward with the project, or in laymen's terms he got "cold feet."

Let's rewind. Here is how it all went down.

Bobby called me the morning the story broke in the media and he was baffled! He was confused! His voice was all low and he sounded wounded. I had never heard him like that before. First of all, he wanted to know how the story got leaked into the press. Second, he was dealing with how Whitney and their daughter Bobbi Kris were feeling about yet another negative outburst of publicity drama about their family, and this time it was rightfully caused by him. I don't think he was really ready for what had just happened! Especially since him and Whitney had just started to heal and become friends after their divorce. We had discussed before how he was fully supportive of Whitney's attempt to make a comeback in the music industry. (In my opinion) I don't think he wanted the pessimistic reports from the book and tabloid gossip to overshadow the fact that Whitney was finally clean, sober, healthy, and happy!

I spent days at a time over a year with Bobby and conducted several long hours of recorded interviews with him. I then took other resources in addition to spending quality time with his family members to come up with the manuscript for this book.

I had been known in the past to do handshake deals with former business partners, especially if they were friends or close associates of mine. This project was no different. Bobby and his family were close friends so we started working on the manuscript with only a handshake deal in place. We decided we would wait until we were about to release the project to bring the attorneys in to complete a final agreement. After about a year, we finished the manuscript. He read and approved the final draft so we initiated talks with our attorneys about finalizing an agreement (as planned). Out of nowhere, quotes were leaked and the stories broke in various countries simultaneously. This is when the media frenzy began and things rapidly went left!

Inconspicuously, Bobby started stalling! The first sign of the fact that was unfolding daily was when he let our first release date of May 13th that we set come and go! He showed no signs of finalizing an agreement. When he let our second release date of June 1st roll around and we still hadn't reached an agreement, it became transparent. Obviously, he was procrastinating! It seemed like him, his manager and his attorneys were trying to find anything that they could to not get the deal done, than to get the deal done! At this point, it started to feel like a conspiracy!

I had heard rumors that Whitney was trying to stop this book from coming out and that she was going to do whatever she had to do to keep it from being published. I started to wonder if Bobby's attorney and/or manager had been paid off by Whitney's people. After all, they were the ones making it difficult for us to reach an agreement. I then started to wonder if Bobby had been influenced by Whitney not to go through with it. Whitney has been known, is known and will always be known as having a major influence on him. For whatever reasons, Bobby, his lawyer and manager were not in a hurry to finalize the agreed-upon book release deadlines!

What started out as a clean-cut, tell-all book of Bobby Brown's life ended up being a negative media circus. For two weeks, the media picked the manuscript apart concentrating on anything they felt could make them be the first to disclose the dirt on Bobby Brown. Inevitably, this could discourage anyone, and in this case maybe Bobby.

Whatever the case, Bobby left me and my distributor standing still. He left us no choice! We didn't know which way to go next because he just started procrastinating. With all of the hard work, time and dedication to the project and money spent out of my pocket preparing this memoir, I decided to make the necessary changes to release it. I made the changes to revise the book so that it reads as a biography in lieu of an autobiography.

All in all, there are no hard feelings from me. At the end of the day, business is business! Maybe Bobby does not want his personal life and the lives of those who matter the most, his family, to be scrutinized and splattered across the televisions, newspapers and websites of America anymore. Maybe he just wants to be left alone. Who knows, I might've done the same thing myself. I can't imagine what it would be like to live under a microscope and every word I say being used against me. I might crack under the pressure too, especially when the attacks are against loved ones. Actor Robert Downey Jr., who has had a public controversial life of drugs like Bobby, has recently done something similar with his book deal. He took a major advance from Harper Collins Publishing, held the money for over two years, then for some reason decided to return the money and back out of the deal.

The call I made on moving on with the release of the book unauthorized was nothing personal, it was strictly business. I will make sure Bobby is still fairly compensated, but I have to move on. Besides money, time, and energy, from a business standpoint, I feel like you can't dangle a project in the public's face by putting it on the market, have over a hundred thousand pre-orders, have all the major wholesale and retail stores waiting on the edge of their seats for a solid release date. Then for personal or whatever reasons decide not to go through with it. That is bad business! That could jeopardize the integrity of my company and damage my business relationships before I even get off the ground. There is too much at stake to just drop the ball. I have really good future projects waiting to be released and this is only one of them. I am the biographer/publisher of the stars and it's my duty to deliver the public good and accurate projects in a timely fashion. I will keep up with my end of the bargain and do just that. So from me, I give to you Bobby Brown: The Truth, The Whole Truth, and Nothing But..., Enjoy!!!!

Prologue

Bobby is one of the greatest entertainers in the world. He has had a successful career over the last few decades. He is a legend and a pioneer of Hip-Hop/R&B and has been an inspiration for most of the young R&B singers today. Just like James Brown set the stage for the great performers like Michael Jackson and Prince that followed him, Bobby's style and performances have become a model for the new generation to follow.

Writing this book about Bobby was very entertaining. We've known each other for years, and he is one of the most interesting people that I have ever met. He has lived a life that people can only dream of. He's met with some of the most famous and powerful people in the world. He's lived the lifestyle of the rich and famous and has dated some of the biggest stars in Hollywood.

Bobby is one of the most misunderstood celebrities in the industry. The media has painted this picture about his personality that makes people think he's a monster. This is the furthest thing from the truth. He has had some trials and tribulations. He's dealt with drug abuse and has had his fair share of run-ins with the law. However, for the most part, people would be surprised to know he is one on the most respectful, generous, and chivalrous guys I know. As for the "bad boy" thing, everyone has that side of them; that if they're rubbed the wrong way, they can be ugly. That is just a part of our personality make-up. Knowing this, I thought it would be a good idea to do some research to get more in depth insight on why we as people behave the way we do. Maybe this would help shed some light on Bobby's psyche and why his life and career was so tumultuous.

Upon completing my studies, I found out that the majority of our personality design can be found in our zodiac sign. I discovered that astrology is a powerful tool for recording associations in life and attempting to understand people's personalities. It provides a model showing the potential for the coming together as a whole of all levels of being. With astrology, we can examine our personal problems and assess the proper solution based on our zodiac sign. It has been used by psychologists over the years as a tool for working with personal experiences. It was an instrument for many great men with brilliant minds like Benjamin Franklin, Galileo, and Carl Jung.

Bobby is an Aquarius born February 5th. This sign represents the water carrier, a man flying in the air who is pouring water. The planet Uranus rules the Aquarius born on this date. The Uranus Aquarius is unpredictable and erratic, marked by sudden bursts of energy, inspiration, and creativity. They work almost by surprise. Their lives are disrupted by sudden, radical, lightning-quick changes. This can be good or bad.

Aquarius' are inherently curious about everything. Despite reserves of energy, the urge to keep constantly busy and mentally occupied puts a lot of stress on their nervous system. They are original thinkers that love to experiment who also have an extremely low threshold for boredom and dull routine. This could possibly explain Bobby's desire to use drugs. It's that same penchant for curiosity, the urge to stay busy, and the low threshold for boredom and experimentation that, if used negatively, can send a person into a world of drugs.

The planet Uranus represents the lightning bolt, which is both inspiration and destruction. When it comes to inspiration, Aquarius' can be very inspiring and have an influence on the whole world like Oprah Winfrey and Michael Jordan, both of whom are Aquarius'. When it comes to destruction, they can be very destructive and their own worst enemy like Bobby and his favorite music star Rick James, who also abused drugs and had a tumultuous career.

On one hand, an Aquarius can be very friendly and humanitarian. They are referred to as geniuses, visionary types, and groundbreakers. However, on the other hand, they can be unemotional, detached, chaotic, and rebellious which could explain a lot of Bobby's behavior and experiences.

While looking for some answers in the astrological heavens, I came up with my own theory. I figured that at least 75 percent of the way people are has to do with their zodiac sign; 10 percent is the environment they grew up in or their background; 10 percent is their genetic make-up; and the other 5 percent encompasses extracurricular activities that can have an effect on the rational thinking process, just like the eggs frying in the pan on the "say no to drugs" commercial… "This is your brain on drugs." I think altogether these are the things that make up the personality of man and give him character. I'm not a scientist or an astrologer, but in my opinion, through self-evaluation, this can be a barometer to explain certain behavior patterns.

Table of Contents

Chapter 1

The Bad Boy of Boston . . .

"Straight from the Hood"

Family First

Ma, Pops, & More

In the beginning there was Robert Barrisford Brown, known to the world as Bobby Brown. He "BE"came into this world on February 5, 1969. On this day, there was a sequence of catastrophic events. There were two killer tornados in Iowa, a hurricane in the Atlantic, an earthquake in California, a major flood in Georgia, and a volcanic eruption at Mount Saint Helens. I think he kind of shook the world (just kidding).On a serious note, he was born in a blizzard, if that means anything. He grew up in the inner-city projects of Orchard Park in Roxbury, Massachusetts. He was the youngest boy of Carol and Herbert Brown with four sisters, Elizabeth ("Bethy"), Anita ("Tina"), Leola ("Lee Lee"), and Carole ("Coupe"), and one brother, Tommy.

His mother was a substitute teacher and homemaker. She substituted at his school whenever they needed her. One day she would be at his school teaching and the next day she'd be at home cleaning and preparing my favorite meals. He especially loved it when she cooked collard greens and cornbread. He could never get enough. He always thought she was the best soul-food cook on the planet. He'd lick his fingers and eat until the plate was clean.

His father was a construction worker who worked hard to feed their family. He'd work all week and drink on the weekend. When he drank, he liked to entertain the family. He'd pull out his guitar and start playing like Chuck Berry. As a matter of fact, he looked like Chuck Berry. Sometimes Bobby even thought he was Chuck Berry. He'd get so wrapped up in his act he could fool you.

Growing up in Bobby's house, you could always smell the aroma of a good home-cooked meal coming from the kitchen. You would also hear the sounds of a James Brown tune playing on the stereo while his mom and dad sang along as if they were his background singers. This was a typical day in the Brown residence.

His parents were music lovers. They always had good music playing in their house. It was always the blues and good ol' soul songs that had real feeling like Donnie Hathaway and the O'Jays. As a matter of fact, Bobby believed his ability to perform came from his parents. Although he had never seen them perform live on stage, he'd seen them perform around the house, act crazy, and be themselves around him, which had an effect on him and turned him into a music lover.

He had his first taste of performing in front of a crowd at the age of four. His mother put him on a stage during the intermission of a James Brown concert at the Sugar Shack in Boston. He wasn't nervous or shy. He started doing his James Brown impression, and the crowd went bananas. At that moment, he knew this was what he wanted to do forever.

By the age of five, it was like he already knew he was gonna be a star. He went by the name of Flash B. And when it came to wardrobe, he believed in being flashy. He would take all of his clothes and put glitter on them. His shirts would have "Flash B" written in glitter on the back. He'd take all of his new shoes and put stars and glitter on them also. His mom would have a fit because she'd buy him a brand new pair of Nikes and you wouldn't even be able to tell they were Nike because he'd put glittered stars all over them. His family tells him to this very day that they knew there was something special about him because he always went that extra mile to do something unique.

He became known to his family as the performer. He performed every chance he got. Their house was the neighborhood spot where there was always a chance for him to do his thing. He would be the center attraction at his parents' card games and things like that. They were a big family that always hosted parties at their house. He would put on his costumes and dance like he was on stage in front of thousands at Madison Square Garden when in reality he was performing in front of a few of his parents' friends in the Orchard Park housing projects, better known as Beirut.

Growing up in the Orchard Park projects was very rough. They were called Beirut by outsiders who feared to come near the area because of its reputation for being killing grounds. Bobby lost a lot of friends to murder. He called them casualties of war because Orchard Park was like a battlefield where only the strong survived. There was one close friend in particular, Jimmy, who got killed in the projects when Bobby was ten. That incident left a bad taste in his mouth and let him know that was a place he never wanted to come back to once he left.

Bobby got shot once when he was twelve. He still has the scar on his right knee. "I had been at a party dancing with some guy's girlfriend when all of a sudden she said, 'You better run! That's my boyfriend!'" says Bobby. "I was like, 'Why are you just now telling me that?' It was too late." He always had dreams of getting out of the ghetto. Ever since he was a kid, his mom would talk to him about how growing up in his environment he could end up dead or in jail. But she told him if he worked hard and kept faith in God he could get out of the ghetto. He was determined to do just that!

He became very active doing any and everything he could do to work toward getting his family out of the ghetto. He did everything from playing basketball and hockey to boxing and working on his musical craft. He did anything to make a difference. In boxing, he was a Golden Gloves champion with seventeen straight knockouts. That was the beginning of the bad boy being born.

Bobby wasn't the only talented sibling in his family. His youngest sister, Carole, was just as talented as him. She was a dancer and a rapper. Actually, her group beat one of his groups in a talent show, which kind of scared him.

Carole and Bobby were very close growing up. They were the two youngest. He was the youngest boy, and she was the youngest girl. They both had a thing for video games. Their favorite games were Pac-Man and Centipede. They were always late for school because they'd stop at the local convenience store and play games early in the morning. Either she'd be on

Pac-Man and he'd be on Centipede, or it would be the other way around. Either way it went, all the kids used to be mad because they would hold up the games until it was time to go to school. It used to get so bad sometimes that the foreign storeowner would have to run them out. He'd always shoo them, "Leave game alone, leave game alone! Go to school!" To this very day, he still loves video games.

In his family, it was all about fun, music, and games. He has a real funny family. So growing up there was a lot of laughter in their house—a lot of being silly, and his mother was the ringleader. She was hilarious. They always had a lot of fun. No matter what was going on in their lives, they always found a reason to laugh. And what's really crazy is everyone in his family has the same laugh. It's in their genes, even their kids have the same laugh. Maybe, just maybe it has something to do with them being a very close and supportive family. I believe that a family that has been through the bad together should be able to share a laugh together.

When Bobby was growing up, his family always supported him in whatever he did. At first, he had to do the dishes like everybody else. His sisters would make him do their chores, and when his brother wasn't around, he had to do his chores, too. But when he started making money, he was like the champ. You know how the champ was always the one everybody praised: "Watch out for Bobby's feet." In the family, he became that guy!

His biggest supporter of them all was his mother. As the years rolled on, she eventually became his manager and confidant who guided him through his career. She was always there to give him words of wisdom and put him back on the right track when he got off. She was a blessing.

But enough about his family. I know what people really want to hear. You want to get all up in his business. So come on, let's get it on!

Making the Music

The Entertainer Within

The first time Bobby remembers being serious about dancing and singing, he was seven years old. He would do whatever dances were popular at the time, popping, locking, breaking, whatever. But it wasn't until he started doing choreography for the other kids in the projects that he found out he had a knack for putting together talent.

By the time he was nine years old, he started putting together groups. His first groups were Bobby and the Angels and the Intruders. He was twelve when he started the group that made him who he is today, New Edition.

New Edition was formed by Michael Bivins and Bobby. In the beginning, there were only four members. He asked Michael to join the group because he was one of the more popular kids on one side of the projects. Mike asked Ricky Bell and Ralph Tresvant who were popular kids on the other side of the projects. Ronnie Devoe didn't join the group until later.

Bobby always dreamed of being a star. He always knew that one day it was going to happen. Sometimes during rehearsal with New Edition, they would watch *Soul Train*. He used to tell them, "One day we're going to be on here." They'd laugh and Bobby would get mad. At that time, he was the only one taking it serious. The other guys did it for talent shows and for something to do after school.

While rehearsing, they would put together routines on whatever the hottest single was at the time. The song that they won a lot of talent shows with was L.T.D.'s "Holding On." They also did Jackson 5 covers that eventually ended up becoming their niche and molded their future.

He was the lead singer of the group in the beginning, but after he heard Ralph's voice, he was like, "You sing lead, and I'll sing 'sometimes.'" Ralph sounded just like Michael Jackson, and Bobby praised Michael Jackson; that was enough for him.

He always had a love for singing, but it was dancing that he was really into. He always has and always will be a dancer first. Dancing to him is what makes an artist a true performer. If an artist just stands in one place and sings, he is only connecting with the audience on one level. But when he dances and sings he is connecting with the audience on all levels. He is giving the crowd all of his energy. This is what made James Brown and Michael Jackson two of the greatest entertainers in the world. They were great dancers and singers who connected with the crowd on every level. Bobby understood this.

New Edition talent shows were all about dancing. They were very successful, always placing in the top three in all the contests. Their stage presence was very strong, and their choreography was always on point, thanks to Bobby. Even though the rest of the guys contributed their input to their dance moves, Bobby always came and added that extra flavor to give them that edge.

The bulk of New Edition's success came from preparation. They'd rehearse for two or three hours a day, five days a week. While other kids were outside playing, they were putting a lot of time into their craft. Although the rest of the guys in the group couldn't see the vision, they always came in and did their part as if they were being moved by a higher power.

Little did they all know they were on to something big. Even though they couldn't see it, stars were on the rise!

Dancing to Get the Deal

On Their Way Up

Dancing always came natural to Bobby. He never had any technical training or anything, but he grew up watching James Brown, Michael Jackson, Prince, and his favorite artist of them all, Rick James. These were some of the guys who influenced him.

Rick James in particular had a career that was similar to his. He was a very big star of his era who liked to party like a rock star. He was a rebel like Bobby because he didn't mind making songs that represented his lifestyle. Songs like "Super Freak" and "Mary Jane" (a song that made reference to marijuana) definitely made statements like Bobby's songs "My Prerogative" and "Humpin' Around." Whereas a lot of celebrities fly under the radar and the world never really gets to hear about their habits and fantasies, Rick and Bobby allowed their lifestyles to play out in the public.

Dancing in talent shows was definitely the basis of Bobby's success. What people don't know is that he started off doing talent shows by himself. His father would give him his allowance, and he would go and enter this talent show on Dudley Street, which was across the street from his projects. Back then, it cost about three or four dollars to enter the contest. He would always come in first or second place. He had to bring his "A game" to these competitions because it was always the best of the best in the city competing. His main competition was a guy named Brook. Brook was a member of two groups. One was *The Transitions,* who were great, and the other was the *Untouchables,* who were like their name: untouchable. Although they would come out there all perfect with their uniforms on and move the crowd, Bobby gave them a lot of trouble.

As a matter of fact, his solo performance in the contests on Dudley Street are what caught the attention of Maurice Starr. At that time, Maurice Starr was a very successful promoter in Boston who used to promote all the talent shows. He had been seeing Bobby perform at different shows and bust his butt to win. He eventually won the preliminaries in the Dudley Street Competition, which landed him a spot in the finals, the Hollywood Talent Night.

After he won that contest, Maurice said, "It'd be good if you had some guys dancing behind you, man." And that's when he brought the members of New Edition on board. As fate would have it, that might have been one of the best moves he's ever made. Bringing the guys to the table didn't turn out to be a bad idea.

Entering the Hollywood Talent Night with them brought them a second-place trophy and a record deal with Maurice's independent label, Streetwise Records. Maurice thought the group would be better with five guys. He wanted one singing and four in the back stepping, as opposed to one singing and three stepping. He figured that would even out the group. That's when their manager at the time, Brooke Payne, brought in his nephew, Ronnie Devoe. This completed the five original members of New Edition known and loved by the world today. Making Ronnie the fifth member turned out to be a good thing because they didn't know that they were getting one of the best dancers and steppers in the group.

Finally seeing them as a five-man group, Maurice thought they should grow Afros and change their name to Majic 5 (which obviously didn't happen). Bobby thought Maurice was in Joe Jackson mode and had this vision of resurrecting the Jackson 5, which they didn't have a problem with because New Edition loved the Jackson 5.

Signing their deal with Maurice didn't put any money in their pockets, and I do mean "NOT Any Money!" "What it did do was give us an opportunity to record an album, which at that time meant more to me than anything," remembers Bobby. "It gave me the opportunity to perform. I loved being in front of a crowd. Hearing the girls scream, seeing different cities, having different experiences, and going through different changes in my life . . . my whole pay was that."

After signing them, Maurice realized that they all were songwriters as well as performers. He allowed them to go in the studio and record some of the songs that they had already written. Two of the first songs they recorded were "Jealous Girl" and then "Candy Girl." "Jealous Girl" was always one of Bobby's favorites because he wrote it. He felt like he got ripped off on that song, but that's another story.

Eventually, Maurice picked "Candy Girl" as their first single and released it in the United Kingdom. It went to number one on their charts, which set up their deal with MCA Records. They went on to finish recording their debut album, *Candy Girl,* and released it in the United States. This album ended up spinning off a few chart-topping singles, "Candy Girl," "Jealous Girl," "Popcorn Love," and "Is This the End," which sold over two million copies.

With their newfound fame as a group, they all

added whatever they had to contribute to make it work. When it came to things like picking out clothes and stuff, they would take a vote. They voted on everything. If one of them wanted to do something, then the others would have to agree. If it was two against two, the fifth member would have to break the tie. In most cases it was Ronnie. He always had the last vote, which is what made him so important to the group. You usually had Mike and Bobby on one side and Ricky and Ralph on the other, and Ronnie always chose Mike and Bobby. "He knew that we were right about most things, especially when it came to dressing," Bobby boasts. "Ricky and Ralph couldn't dress at all!"

New Edition was all about being flashy! They always wore shiny suits or some type of fancy outfit. They would hit the stage decked out in glittered suits and bow ties. They most definitely stood out amongst all the other artists at that time and made it their business to steal the show every chance they got.

As far as Bobby was concerned they had finally made it to the big time. Now it was time to show the world what they had to offer!

Chapter 2

New Edition around the World . . .

"From Orchard Park to Japan"

The New Jackson 5

"We Made It"

The guys first days on the road as New Edition were very interesting. They traveled from city to city in a station wagon. Imagine six or seven guys at a time being stuffed in a five-passenger wagon with the storage space in the back. Someone was always stuck with the displeasure of having to lie down in the back, which left him in an awkward position for the ride. They always found themselves racing to the car to try to get a seat. The last person to the car had to take the uncomfortable ride.

It wasn't until they got new management that they started traveling on tour buses, which were homes on wheels. On the weekends they'd get on the bus and go to work. Sometimes they'd do five shows in one night. When they went to New York, they would play every borough: Brooklyn, Queens, Staten Island, Bronx, and Manhattan. They would hit every club in that area.

By Sunday night they were back on the bus, and on Monday morning they were dropped off at school.

During that time, school was kind of rough for them. With the long hours on the road they would arrive at school exhausted. Sometimes they got in trouble for falling asleep in class, missing assignments, or not completing homework.

What helped out is that they had a song on the radio, so they always got support and leniency from some of the school staff, but for the most part Boston's school system didn't play that. At times, some of the students would complain because they got special treatment. They eventually got tutors, but that didn't come until the second album. It was all about the girls when they first started touring. The girls would do some pretty crazy things. They would wait for them in their hotel lobbies, so they had to sneak out the back doors to avoid them. Sometimes they had decoys to try to throw the girls off. A lot of times it didn't work. The girls were pretty smart. They would pay the hotel staff or convince them to give up information.

Bobby has been offered everything from money to expensive gifts to spend time with girls. Sometimes when he wasn't busy, he'd take the time to go out with fans, just to show his appreciation. Even girls' parents used to make offers to New Edition security to meet group members. Once a doctor offered their security $100 for his daughter to stay an hour in Ralph's room.

There were also frantic little girls that used to pee their pants when they met them. They would scream, fall out in the floor, and get extremely dramatic! It was always chaos. Everywhere they went they got mobbed. They couldn't even walk into a mall without getting chased out.

They didn't really have time for girlfriends back then. They all had a few special people they talked to on the phone from time to time, but they were too busy for serious relationships.

In addition to having plenty of girls, they used to do some crazy things on tour. They were young and from the ghetto, so they would do things like go into the bathroom and smoke cigarettes and joints. They'd buy BB guns and shoot up the hotel. They were just mischievous. They got kicked out of every place they went. They carried on like rock stars because that's what they thought rock stars did.

Their behavior offstage was wild and crazy, but once they hit the stage they were totally different characters. It was all GOOD then! They patterned themselves after the Jackson 5. In fact, they emulated everything they did. The Jackson 5 became successful because of who they were individually, so they all picked out a member of the group to impersonate. "Of course, three of us fought over being Michael," said Bobby. "Ralph, Ricky, and I were the ones who wanted to be Michael, and believe it or not, Ronnie completely wanted to be Randy and that's it, the bongo guy."

The whole time they were on tour, they totally imitated the Jackson 5. They were going through shows doing their routines just like they did when they competed in talent shows. It was like they were being someone that they weren't, but it was fun and it worked! Eventually, they were comfortable with adding their own flavor. You could still tell they were influenced by the Jackson 5, but they were determined to do something groundbreaking and new. They were definitely on their way to becoming the "New Jackson Five!"

This, of course, made meeting Michael Jackson one of the highlights of their career. Michael invited them to his house. Bobby remembers being very excited. All he could think was, "We've been invited to MJ's house. This was confirmation that they had made it!" This was pre-Neverland Ranch days, so he didn't have the amusement park, zoo, or the other things all the kids loved. Bobby still remembers when they pulled up at his house, they were all like, "WOW! Look at this house!" It looked like a castle. They had never been exposed to that type of environment, so going there was like going on a field trip. They were all starstruck when they walked in the house.

Although meeting Michael was extremely exciting for them, the most interesting thing to Bobby was when his sisters, Janet and Latoya, walked in the house. Michael with his light voice said, "Come on guys, let's go play some video games." Bobby being the ladies man that he was, was more interested in finding out what room Janet went in. He'd had a crush on Janet since she played Penny on the hit television show *Good Times*. Even though he didn't get to lay hands on Janet at that time, all the guys in the group did get a chance to smack LaToya on the butt. Michael started playing this game where they were all running through the house. They ran up the stairs and down a hallway. While running down the hallway, guess who was standing there startled: Latoya. Starting with Michael, as they ran by her, they all smacked her on the butt. She just stood there in shock. Bobby was thrilled, "being a teenager and getting to put hands on Latoya Jackson wasn't a bad thing."

Although Bobby thought Michael was flattered by their impression of the Jackson 5 and really enjoyed hanging out with them, he didn't see him again until later on in life at one of Michael's anniversaries celebrating the success of his career.

Life was great! Bobby was living out his dreams. Here is the kid from the ghetto, now in L.A. at Michael Jackson's house and on the road touring the world from Europe to Japan, performing in front of thousands. Whoever came up with the philosophy "Dreams Come True," he can honestly say he's a witness because he was watching his unfold right before his eyes.

Although New Edition's first album was successful, they left Maurice's label, Streetwise Records, and signed directly to MCA Records. That's the politics of this business: "The big man swallows up the little man!" MCA found out that their group was a cash cow, so they decided to move the middleman out of the way.

Maurice didn't take this too lightly. He felt that the group betrayed him for leaving his label. He started doing things to try to hurt them. They were served court papers on a regular basis. He went as far as suing them for the name *New Edition*. He didn't win though. Their manager, Brooke Payne, had given them that name before they met Maurice.

After leaving Streetwise records, they started working on their second album. This was their self-titled album, *New Edition*. They could automatically tell the difference between being signed directly to MCA versus being on Streetwise Records. Their recording budgets were a lot larger. They were recording in studios that were so lavish they could have made them their home. Their video budgets were increased tremendously also. They now had videos with special effects. The "My Secret" video even had exclusive footage from the L.A. Lakers. They could definitely feel the difference; they felt the star POWER!

New Edition was on top. Their second album was a major success. They added a string of additional hits to their catalog. Songs like, "Cool It Now," "Mr. Telephone Man," and "My Secret" solidified their celebrity. They were now a force to be reckoned with in the industry.

Earning the Title

Competition in the Group

When you are in a group, there is a lot of competition among the members. Everyone is trying to stand out and get his individual shine. There are some members that get along and others that don't. Or you're cool with one member this day and fighting with him the next. It's pretty much like growing up with brothers and sisters and having sibling rivalries.

While in New Edition, Mike and Bobby were really close in the beginning. He was least close to Ricky because they always bumped heads on creative issues. By the time they got their deal and started touring, he started getting closer to Ralph because they were usually the ones that got pointed out for doing certain things, especially some of the things they did on stage. The other guys used to get mad because Ralph and Bobby did anything it took to hype up the crowd. They would step outside of their routines, go to the side of the stage, and pump their hips to the crowd while they were still stepping. The girls would start roaring, and that's all Bobby wanted to hear. If he could hear the crowd scream, then that was a successful show to him. Ralph also did these types of things.

Bobby explains, "The other guys in the group used to tell me and Ralph after some of the shows, 'Man, that show sucked!' I would be like, 'Screw ya'll. I had a good time! I had the crowd screaming; the crowd screamed for me. I don't know about you, but I had a good show!'" This would cause a real fistfight.

On the road they also fought over different things like what they would wear on stage. They all wore different colors. One person would have on blue, the other green, etc. Bobby always picked red. Although they knew that was Bobby's color, the other guys would try to wear red also. Of course, this would cause confusion. He never could understand their rationale. If they knew his favorite color was red and that he was going to put up a fight if they tried to wear it, why would they try to put on red every other week? He thought this was ridiculous!

Clothes were not the only thing that caused a problem. They fought over using each other's hair products or not putting their initials on their jock straps, stuff like that. Bobby also thought the guys were always jealous of his hair because it was curly. He recalls, "Michael and I also had curly hair, but everybody else's hair was screwed up. I'm talking about knotty, nappy hair. Let's not forget about Ralph's ducktail. I guess it worked back then, but looking back at old videos, he looked like a cartoon character."

One thing they didn't have to fight over was the girls. Everybody basically got their equal share of people who liked them. Bobby found out from a survey that more girls had his poster up in their rooms than any of the other guys.

When it came to their shows, they would fight Ralph all the time because the screams he'd get were a little louder and more intense since he led the group. What this did was make all the other guys in the group want to sing lead. "The guys would pout, 'I'm tired of this; I want to sing a song too,'" remembers Bobby. "Everybody got to the point where they wanted to sing a song. When we got into the studio everybody got a fair chance. We'd be like, 'Go ahead and sing it,' and when they didn't get it right, we'd be like, 'Okay, you didn't sing it right.' This caused them to miss their chance at getting the lead." Inevitably, Ricky and Bobby, being the only other lead singers in the group besides Ralph, would fight over what other parts they were going to do on the song.

Although Ralph got the most attention from the girls, personally, Bobby thought if they hollered for anyone after Ralph it was him. Actually, it didn't really matter to him because he felt the older women liked him anyway. "While Ralph had the teeny-boppers, I had their mothers."

It's been said that a little friendly competition has never hurt anybody. New Edition's future looked bright, but just like every other successful group that has come along, like the Temptations and Supremes to name a few, members start to have differences that can eventually take a toll on the group. As history has revealed, these differences never turn out good, and eventually someone leaves the group.

Going Solo

The Show Must Go On

Bobby always thought he quit New Edition. It wasn't until twenty years later on a VH-1 New Edition special that he found out otherwise. To his surprise, they disclosed they had actually voted him out of the group.

His mother and his brother Tommy had started managing his solo career, so they were handling all of his business at the time. For whatever reason, they never told him that the group had voted him out. He was walking around all cocky thinking, "How you feel boys? I quit the group." And then years later he found out they had actually voted him out on a three-to-one vote. To this day, he still doesn't know who the three were that wanted him out or who the one was that had his back. He's been trying to find that out for years, and not one of them will tell the truth. But out of everybody, for some reason, he feels that Ricky was definitely one of those three.

Bobby believes their management team at the time, Jump and Shoot (Rick Smith, Stevie Shocks, and Bill Durham), had a lot to do with the guys' voting him out. He came to find out management had been telling the guys that he was selling and using drugs and doing too many things that could negatively affect the group's image.

For the most part, he thinks management had it out for him because he was the rebellious one in the group that didn't go for "anything." He didn't let them piss on him and tell him it was raining! He would always question their judgment and actions. After touring for a while, he started to realize they were selling out shows all over the country, but they were still broke. He and his mother had talks about these kinds of things because she felt it wasn't right. "It was almost like we were some whores getting pimped," says Bobby. "Coming off the road, the tour bus would drop us back off in the projects, and we were back to our reality — poor, struggling project kids. I had a serious problem with this, but the other guys didn't see it. I brought it up in a meeting: why were we getting paid a salary of $120 a week while our managers were getting the bulk? The guys got mad because they thought I was trying to screw things up. This is when I started to pull away from the group. I had come to the conclusion that until they could see what I was seeing, we could not be friends."

Because of his antics, his last days with New Edition were kind of rocky. The other guys were getting fed up at their concerts; Bobby would completely take over the show. He was tired of them making him look like he was always the bad guy. So he started conducting himself as such. They argued after almost every show. The guys constantly bickered about how he was messing up the performances by not being in sync or how he was interfering with the routine. At that point, he didn't really care anymore. He knew he was going solo, so he just started singing his own stuff and doing his own thing. They would be in the middle of a song, and he'd break out into an extended remix, adlibbing for an extra ten minutes, dragging out the set. Basically, he stole the show. This is something that naturally happened when they performed because of his dancing skills, but at this point, he had taken it to another level. The guys would be FURIOUS!

Then on one particular night it all came to a head. Mike and Bobby got into a scuffle on the stage. Bobby threw a microphone stand at him, walked back to the dressing room, took off his clothes, and put on a robe, and then came back out and blew the crowd away. He walked off that stage feeling like he had what it took to control a crowd by himself. He decided he didn't need to go through the bull with them or management anymore. This was the last show he did with them.

Regardless of whether he got kicked out or quit the group, it didn't matter who snubbed whom. From the beginning, he always knew he was going to go solo. It was a big plan of his. He was using New Edition as a stepping stone. To compete in the Hollywood Talent Night, he needed a group. Maurice Starr was looking for the next Jackson 5, so he gave him what he wanted. He always knew he was going to go back to doing his own thing since he started off solo. While he was in the group, he continued to write songs for his solo project. He was going in the studio with different producers, preparing himself for what was to come.

By the time he left New Edition he had finished recording his solo album and had signed to a solo deal with MCA Records, the same label that New Edition was signed to.

His solo career had already been planned out by MCA Records. The head executives of the label at the time, Jheryl Busby and Ernie Singleton, put it all together. Jheryl Busby sat him and his mother down at Carney's, the famous train hot-dog stand in New York. He told him that they really loved the material that he recorded and that they were excited about signing him to a solo deal.

MCA always knew that Bobby was a different type of performer than the other members of the group. They felt like he had a more grown-up, mature type of appeal. So they strategically planned to market this album to a totally different audience.

Upon him leaving New Edition, there were a lot of doubts circulating around the industry. People were saying, "Bobby's not going to make it. He made the worst mistake of his life leaving New Edition." They were being negative, which has always motivated him to succeed. He has always welcomed the "haters." They give him more ammunition! They fuel his fire! Eventually, he proved them all wrong.

Upon signing his solo deal, he got an advance of $250,000. He finally got an opportunity to do something for his mother that he always wanted to do, and that was to get her out of the projects. All his life, all he ever heard was his mother complain to his dad, "When are you gonna buy me a house? You promised to move me into a house." So he figured he would step in and help his dad out. He bought his mom a house in the suburbs of Canton, Massachusetts. It was a nice house in a conservative community. This was definitely a change for his family. The air was different. Now they could sleep peacefully at night without wondering if a stray bullet was going to come through the window.

His first album, *The King of Stage,* released in 1987, did pretty well. He landed a hit with the number-one R&B single "Girlfriend," and the album went gold. Back then in the late eighties, that was considered a very successful album. Unlike the industry today, success was measured by your having a number-one single. If you had a number-one single and you went gold, you were a success.

Along with himself, he had some of the greatest writers and producers to help him do the album. He had Larry Blackman from Cameo and Larry White, to name a couple.

By the time he started working on his second album, *Don't Be Cruel,* the only person in New Edition that he was in contact with was Ralph. "I would play my album for Ralph, and Ralph would go back and tell the group, 'Man, his songs are good; we gotta do songs like that!'"

What was happening is the sound of the music industry was changing, and it was changing into Bobby's sound. On his second album, he worked with the New Jack Swing producer Teddy Riley and R&B producers LA Reid and Babyface. However, New Edition was still doing the bubble gum stuff like "Popcorn Love."

New Edition was dying out around this time, and Bobby felt they were threatened by his solo success. They knew that the crowd was feeling him as a solo artist and that he was the New Kid on the Block. They would do things like choose other people over him to open their shows. On one occasion Bobby complained, "They made me the opening act and chose Al B. Sure to come on just before them on their headlining tour, knowing that I would clearly bust his chops. They knew that I would bust their chops too. If I came on just before them, they knew that the energy from my performance would definitely take away from their show." It was things like this that kept a distance between them.

New Edition was definitely turning into his competition. When they saw his style maturing, they went in the studio and put together a mature album. This brought about the *Heartbreak* album released at the end of 1988 with Johnny Gill (Bobby's replacement, for those of you who don't know).

Although the *Heartbreak* album did well, it couldn't compare to the success of Bobby's second album, *Don't Be Cruel,* which was released in the summer of 1988. This album sold 11.5 million copies worldwide and another 5 million copies on the remix album, *Dance! . . . Ya Know It!"* During this time R&B artists did not sell albums in record-breaking numbers like this. This was definitely a deviation from the norm. This made Bobby a Super Star! Or shall I say Rock Star because when an urban artist crosses over into the pop world and sells the kind of records he sold, that puts him in a whole different category.

Critics started comparing *Don't Be Cruel* to his first album, *King of Stage.* They stated that his career started off slow. Well of course, everyone would feel like his first album wasn't as successful when *Don't Be Cruel* came out and sold enough albums to destroy any negative thoughts or doubts the critics ever had about him.

Don't Be Cruel was a very special album to him. It had so many great songs on there he couldn't just pick one that he liked the best. With top-ten hits like "Don't Be Cruel," "My Prerogative," "Roni," "Every Little Step," and "Rock Wit' Cha," it quickly became a classic. "I listened to that album a lot, and I had never done that before with my past albums," recalls Bobby.

The success of *Don't Be Cruel* made some of the other guys from New Edition start to come around. It had been a while since he had spoken with most of them. After his career started to take off, he would gradually see or hear from them one by one. After all that happened, he assumed they figured if you can't beat 'em, join 'em!

Seeing the success of his solo career caused New Edition to go their separate ways and try their luck at solo albums also. Eventually, Ralph went solo and had success with a platinum album. Johnny went solo and had multiplatinum success. Ronnie, Ricky, and Mike started a group called Bell Biv Devoe, and they also had multiplatinum success. Everyone was doing well. They had all worked hard their entire lives, so they deserved it!

They all visited each others' concerts. Most of the time, Bell Biv Devoe and Johnny were on tour together. Bobby would visit them when they came to town. Ralph and Bobby would get together every now and then on a more personal note and go fishing. They were the more family oriented guys from the group who liked the outdoors. They had a few things in common other than music.

Bobby proclaims, "I never got a chance to get New Edition back for all of the things they did to me. All the things I had to go through after finding out on VH-1 that they had actually kicked me out of the group. I don't think I'll ever have a chance to just sit down and talk to them about it. But I want them to know just how much they hurt me but, at the same time, helped me become the man I am today!"

Chapter 3

My Prerogative . . .

"I Made this Money, You Didn't!"

Party Like a Rock Star

Booze, Babes, & Bars

At the height of his career Bobby had been all over the world. He had done everything! He had bought everything! Anything that a person could dream of, he had been there, bought that, and done that!

He used to hang out at all the hot spots all over the world. Any club that was high profile and was the place to be, he was there. You could find him in the VIP busting bottles of expensive champagne. There were so many women around you couldn't even see him. He was hanging out with some of the biggest celebrities in the business: Eddie Murphy, Dennis Rodman, Mike Tyson, and other people of their status. At that time in his career, he always crossed paths with the most successful entertainers out. He was also dating some of the hottest babes in the biz.

He spent a lot of money back in those days. He would go through a hundred thousand dollars in one sitting, whether he was just out one day splurging with friends on a trip or just partying. The sky was the limit! He would spend a million dollars on a shopping spree buying anything from cars, furniture, to clothes. He never thought twice about it when it came down to his wardrobe. He would do crazy things like buy brand new cars and leave them on the side of the road with the keys in the ignition just to see what would happen to it.

When it came to giving back to the community, he did this almost every day. His main charity was giving to the homeless, and he had his own special way of doing this. Whenever he was riding down the street and saw a homeless person, along with himself, he would make anyone he was with empty out their pockets. He didn't care if they had a thousand dollars, he would give that homeless person all of the money they had. Some of his entourage stopped carrying large amounts of cash when they were with him because they knew the procedures once he spotted someone homeless.

Bobby considered money from doing his shows his spending money. During this time he was making two hundred and fifty thousand dollars a show. At one point, he was doing a show almost every night. He would pay all his bills with fifty thousand dollars, and the other two hundred thousand was for him to play with. He made about thirty million dollars over a couple of years. Back then, thirty million was like having fifty million in today's economy. He might've had a lot of problems, but money wasn't one of them!

He bought several cars, a couple of Rolls Royces, some SUVs, and a few Mercedes Benzes. His favorite was a 560 SEL convertible Mercedes Benz. At that time, this was one of the most prestigious cars on the streets.

He had his car shipped all over the States. He always spent long periods of time in different parts of the country. He might be in Atlanta for a couple of months, then L.A. or back home in Boston. He always divided his time up in different cities when he wasn't on tour. He was never the one to be stationary. Wherever he was staying, he had his convertible shipped. Everyone who knew him back then knew that was his "baby." He even used it in the *Don't Be Cruel* video.

The most expensive thing he bought was his two-million-dollar mansion in the upscale area of North Atlanta. He bought this mansion from the Porn King, who was one of the first people to sell porn on VHS. It had all the trappings for a rich bachelor, complete with an Olympic-sized pool, tennis courts, game room, theatre room and guest headquarters. The house sat on a hill away from the street. It had two big lions at the end of the driveway. When you drove toward the house, it looked as if you were approaching Castle Grayskull. It had that spooky effect, which made you think of the movie, *The Omen*. The mansion had all kinds of special features and hidden compartments. There were tunnels in the middle of the walls that Bobby could walk through, go from room to room, and look in without anyone knowing. It was like a 007-type setup.

If walls could talk at that place, they would definitely have a lot to say! Bobby had everything from bikini parties to smoked-out slumber parties. They'd drink and get high from sunup to sundown. He had women that would visit and end up being there for weeks at a time. It was a party day in and day out whenever he was there. It was set up something like the Playboy Mansion, and he was the new Hugh Hefner.

The guest list included the who's who in the entertainment industry. Bobby refuses to go into details about his guest list. "I won't say any names because I'm not a snitch. Being from where I'm from, snitches end up in ditches, so I don't do that. (Those of you who were there, you know who you are.) Everyone knew the rules of the house. 'What happened at the mansion stayed at the mansion!'"

To this very day, Bobby thinks that house was haunted. The Porn King was legendary for being a gangster that made people disappear when he had problems with them. There were stories about women being killed and bodies being buried in that house. There were also stories of millions of dollars being hidden in the trenches of the house. Bobby used to have parties where they would go on a hunt looking for the money. The house was very spooky. "There were nights when I'd get high out of my mind, and ghosts in the form of naked white women would come down from the ceiling and have sex with me," Bobby remembers. "I'm not kidding! Whether it was the drugs or my imagination, or the drugs and my imagination, it didn't matter, it seemed so real and happened so often that I got used to it. I just went along with it like it was just another part of my life."

Back then, a lot of his days were just a blur. He partied so hard sometimes he didn't even know what day it was. Better yet, sometimes he didn't even know what month or year it was. That's what he paid managers for, to keep up with his schedule.

He also bought a lot of things for his family and friends. Whoever was out shopping with him would have a shopping spree too. By now the whole world has heard that he has always taken care of his family. Most of his siblings lived with him and just kind of stuck with him throughout his whole career. They were always a tight family like that. Just like you had "the Waltons," you also had "the Browns!"

In addition to family and celebrity associates, he was known to hang with people from all walks of life. He never really got caught up in the whole bougie Hollywood thing. I guess you can say he's a down-to-earth brother that didn't forget where he came from. Growing up where he grew up, it's kind of hard to forget! I think that's another reason why he is the way he is. You can take a brother out the ghetto, but you can't take the ghetto out the brother. Everybody has heard the phrases "he's acting so ghetto" or "ghetto fabulous." Basically, this just means, it doesn't matter how rich or famous you are, if you come from the ghetto, it is going to show at times. It did with Bobby. He stayed true to who he was. He refused to let money, fortune, or fame change him totally!

Although he had a lot of good times and spent a lot of money, when it was all said and done, he learned a valuable lesson. "After going out, getting drunk, and throwing money around like it was nothing, thinking people around me were my friends, later I realized they weren't," says Bobby. "There were a lot of people just trying to be around me because of my fame and fortune and not to be a true friend. Looking back, I can truly say I could count the genuine friendships I had on one hand. I started to feel like it was safer to be by myself because I was a better friend to myself than I believed other people could be to me."

From Candy Girls to Super Stars

Stars, Models, & More

By the time Bobby reached his third single on the Don't Be Cruel album, he was one of the biggest stars in the world. You know what that means. . ."With success comes the women!" A wise man once said.

"At this time, I probably had dated half of the industry," Bobby admits. "From Janet Jackson to Holly Robinson, from Madonna to the Real Roxanne (the Spanish one) and Karyn White. I met Madonna early in my career. She used to open up shows for New Edition in New York at the beginning of her career. So running back into her and getting to know her better at the height of my success was like a reunion. The list goes on from the who's who to the flavor of the month. These were people that I just dated. I'm not saying anything else. I'm not the one to kiss and tell!"

He continues, "There were also a couple of soap opera stars like Angie from *All My Children* (Debbie Morgan); I dated her once. I also dated some models and actresses. There were rumors going around about Jasmine Guy and me, but we were only friends. The same with Paula Abdul. My relationship with them was more on a friendly basis."

On the other hand, his relationship with Madonna was a little hot and heated. She was once caught seducing him in the back of his limo by one of his bodyguards. She was very aggressive in her pursuit of him.

Out of all the women he dated back then, he was never really serious with any of them. He was only serious with the mother of two of his children, Kim Ward. She stayed down with him throughout all of his first success and never really interfered with him and the other women he dated. Bobby says of Kim, "She used to always tell me, 'They're not gonna keep you in their lives. They're not gonna love you like I do.' But of course I wasn't hearing that. Life was great for me at the time. I wanted and had the best of the best of everything."

Ms. Janet Jackson was the best thing going at the time in the music industry. Bobby had always had a thing for her since seeing her when they visited Michael's house years earlier. During an interview on BET's Donnie Simpson video show, he finally got a chance to let her know how he felt. He had been contemplating whether he should just put it out there or hold back. He decided to do it. When Donnie asked him about his love life, he figured that was his cue. Without hesitating, he said, "I'm in love with Janet Jackson." Not knowing what the response was going to be, he didn't think anything else about it.

Shortly after, Janet called. Bobby confesses he was pretty excited to get the call. He was like, "Yes! She bit!" Getting a call from Janet Jackson during the days of her album *Control* was a pretty big thing. And it didn't hurt that things were going pretty well for him. It was like two celebrities at the top of their games hooking up.

Almost instantly, he and Janet started dating. For their first date they met at a Häagen Dazs ice cream parlor in L.A. She showed up with one of her girlfriends, and they all had ice cream. "I'll never forget," Bobby remembers. "She had strawberry ice cream, and she complained about how she wasn't supposed to be eating it because she was on a diet."

"I really fell for Ms. Jackson," he continues. "I never usually fall for women that fast, but she was an exception. Maybe it had something to do with my childhood crush; or maybe it was because she was one of the finest and most sought after women in the world at the time. I don't know what it was, but she had me 'open!'"

They dated for a while. They saw each other and talked on the phone whenever they could in between their busy schedules. It was hard trying to maintain a relationship since both of them were in the business. Her itinerary sent her to one part of the world, while his to another.

The way their relationship ended kind of broke his heart. "I was telling her that I loved her and wanted her to leave the guy she was with at the time," he admits. "She told me she couldn't and that her family wouldn't allow her to be with a black man. This really shocked me, so I backed off."

After dating Janet, his confidence level shot sky high. He knew that if he could have her, there weren't too many more women out of his league. As far as he was concerned, he felt like he could have had a shot at Elizabeth Taylor, or the Queen of England for that matter. Instead, God had someone just as powerful and just as famous as either one of these ladies. By now everyone in the world should be familiar with their relationship.

My Way or No Way

"Bad Boy" Bobby

Believe it or not, Bobby really didn't start having serious run-ins with the law until he was thirty years old. This whole "Bad Boy" thing didn't escalate until after he got married. Before that, it had only been hinted at by the media. They never really used the term Bad Boy.

After he got married it was like the Bad Boy marries the Pop Princess. All of a sudden, he was termed that because of the royal image that everyone had of his wife at the time, Whitney Houston. Whitney was rich and famous. She was one of the biggest pop stars in the world. She was loved and respected by many and considered to be the All-American Sweetheart. Marrying someone like her put his life under a microscope.

Although he never really got in trouble with the law early in his career, he was guilty of being a little bit rebellious. He's a rebel by nature, a rebel with a cause. He explains, "I've always had this thing like if you rubbed me the wrong way, you shouldn't expect for me to be nice."

The types of things he did that made the news early on were minor. From his conflict with New Edition to a couple of stage incidents, it was nothing really serious. He also had a little reputation for seducing the women on and off the stage. He had a reputation for just being with a lot of women period, which was called being a womanizer. He called it being good with the women. This way of thinking did nothing to help his image. In fact, it was his way of thinking/*or not thinking*, that got him in trouble all the time. Incidents like this caused the whole "Bad Boy" thing to start brewing in the media.

The Bad Boy title that he received was just an image. Just like Mick Jagger or any other rock star, they never really outgrow their images on stage or in the media. However, if you get to know these people on a personal level, then you'll understand who they really are and be able to separate the image from the real person.

For the most part, the real Bobby is like a big kid at heart. Anyone that knows him (or if you've seen his reality show, that's the real him) can tell you that he doesn't take life that seriously. He likes to have fun and enjoy life. He's a free spirit.

On the flipside, he does have this personality that comes out if he feels challenged. I guess you can call this the Bad Boy. He explains, "The term, to me, doesn't necessarily mean that I have to rip your head off or do something illegal. It does set the tone not to look at me as a pushover. I'm definitely going to stand my ground. I've always been a fighter in that sense. I'm a fighter by nature because I was raised in the projects where you had to fight for your life. Not to mention I was a Golden Gloves boxer, just to let you know I'm good with my hands, too. That doesn't mean that I go out looking for trouble or looking to be the aggressor. At the same time, I'm no punk. If trouble comes my way, I deal with it."

"There are plenty of times when I had to stand up to people to let them know that I wasn't going to be handled. My philosophy is, 'If you don't stand for something, you'll fall for anything.' This philosophy took me a long way."

Standing up for himself went as far back as New Edition. He wasn't going to go for some of the things that the other guys went for. He would always speak his mind. If he felt he was right about something, he'd stand behind it.

His whole career, he's always had it out with staff and executives from his label. They always tried to tell him how to live his life. They always wanted to keep tabs on him and control him because he was their meal ticket, but it didn't work. He always ended up doing things the way he wanted.

Just like he said in his song "My Prerogative," "I made this money, you didn't." He's the one held accountable for what he does with his money and his life. At the end of the day, he's going to have to be the one who has to live with the results of his actions. So if he wants to live his life like there's no tomorrow, then he's the one who's gonna have to live with that. Bobby has always displayed this type of attitude throughout his life and career.

He speaks candidly about his ways, "Being the way I am, I have a lot of respect for those in my position who stand up and live their lives according to how they feel and don't worry about what's politically correct."

"I'm not easily impressed with other celebrities," he continues. "But, meeting men like Nelson Mandela and Bishop Tutu were real big moments for me. These men are individuals who have had influences on whole cultures. Not only are they men of honor, but they are men with a cause. Having a cause in life is what moves me the most."

"Another person I was impressed to meet was Mike Tyson. He was a great boxer, and I was a boxer that loved the sport just as much as he did. I can't say exactly what else it was about Mike, but I think I saw myself in him. In my opinion, Mike was and still is to this day a rebel with a cause. He does things how he wants to do them. His prerogative!"

What people don't know is Bobby has always been into having an influence or changing peoples' lives in certain ways, whether it's through music or culture. He is in no way a role model. He is an example to people of "how not to be." He wants people to look at his life and learn from his mistakes.

Bobby is the prime example of the famous quote, "I work hard, I play hard!" If he were to die tomorrow, he would have done more at his young age than your average eighty-year-old man. He can pretty much say he's lived life to the fullest. He's done it all! Most importantly, like Frank Sinatra said, "I did it my way!"

Chapter 4

Impacting the World...

"Paying Tribute to the King"

The King of Stage

Don't Be Cruel Tour

Bobby's been called everything from the King of New Jack Swing to the King of R&B. Those were titles given to him by other people, not ones that he proposed. The title that he has always undoubtedly claimed is the King of Stage!

"I always considered myself the King of Stage. When I was with New Edition, I was the King of that Stage then also. I was the one bringing the excitement to the crowd by the way I performed. I always worked harder to make them scream," Bobby claims.

He continues, "I love the stage. I love everything about it, including its points. There are seven points of a stage, and you have to work all seven. I mastered this technique, which is what made me one of the best performers in the world."

After leaving New Edition, he named his first tour after the title of his first album, The *King of Stage.* This was his first tour as a solo artist. Although this tour wasn't that big compared to his later tours, I think it established him as "The King of Stage." He really got to show his individual skills as a solo act.

Next came the mother of all tours, The *Don't Be Cruel Tour*, which was the biggest tour of his career. He sold out coliseums all over the world, from France to Japan. The stage production on this tour was about the same as on a Michael Jackson or Madonna tour. He was the King of Stage, so he had to live up to it. He had props coming out of the stage, objects flying around, and a crew of dancers that nobody could get with. Early in his career he had Heart & Soul (Derrick and Willie), and later he recruited some fly girls that went by the name of Mecca (Carolyn, Saleema, Merylin, and Shane). Mecca was definitely one of the baddest dance crews to hit the stage, which is why they stayed with him throughout his career. His hype man was Travis. Bobby would change about seven times during one show while Travis rocked the crowd. He had an entourage of about thirty people. One of his life long friends and business partners he grew up with in Boston, Nate Smith, and his brothers Gary and Greg ("Girky") were a part of the crew. They had been with him since the beginning of his New Edition days. His security was no joke either. A.J. Alexander held it down for him wherever they went.

His opening acts were top-ten acts like Levert and Karyn White. They traveled all around the world like the circus. "My favorite places were London and Japan," Bobby recalls. "I really loved Japan. I've been there at least fifty times since then. Every time I go, it gets better and better. They show me a lot of love there. They welcome me with open arms. I've had a chance to eat at the Emperor's Palace, where not too many people are allowed to go. I think this is what makes me love sushi so much. When I am there, they even dress me in warrior outfits. They are just great people."

Although he was recognized as one of the most famous entertainers all around the world, he still considered himself an average Joe. He looked at himself as just plain ol' Bobby, and that's how he's always carried himself. When he was on tour, it was always a problem for his security. He would sneak out of the hotel room by himself and try to walk the streets to see if people would recognize him. This was really hard, because for some reason he would always end up getting chased back to the hotel. Sometimes he tried to go in disguise, and it still wouldn't work. He would have on a hat pulled all the way down to his eyes or a fake beard, all types of covers. "I think it was something about my walk and my expensive clothes and the fact that I didn't choose to leave off my expensive jewelry that gave me away," he professes.

He adds, "My pockets would always have the mumps! (For those of you who are ebonically challenged, that means I had a pocket full of money.) I would stop at stores and just buy up everything. People would recognize me and be like, 'Aren't you Bobby Brown!' From that point, it was over. Once you give one person an autograph, it's like a domino effect. I'd walk out of the store and there would be another thousand people waiting for me, news cameras and all! So I'd have to have someone call my security (this was pre-cell phone days), and security not knowing I had sneaked out would be like, 'No, Bobby's not there; he's in his room.' I'd grab the phone and say, 'Come get me!' My security had a lot of problems with me."

When it came to the women, they came a dime a

dozen. There were always hundreds of women waiting on him at his hotel after shows. Most of the time, he had a method he used when it came to choosing the woman he was going to spend the evening with (or women, depending on how he was feeling that night). He usually picked them out in the crowd during shows and pulled them on stage while he was performing. At that time, he would tell them to meet him at the hotel later. He was Mr. Casanova himself.

Paving the Way

A Living Legend

In Bobby's eyes, he feels that he changed R&B music into what it is today. Although others might think different, as far as he's concerned, he knows he had a lot of influence on the sound of music overall.

The *Don't Be Cruel* album definitely had a major impact on the music industry. It introduced the New Jack Swing sound. It also helped launch the careers of LA Reid, Babyface, and Teddy Riley as superstar producers that controlled the sound of the music industry into the early 90s.

His single "Don't Be Cruel" broke the barriers on the pop airwaves as to their having a song in heavy rotation with rap on it. They made two versions, one with rap and one without. The one without rap was so short they were forced to play the one with rap, which made that version more popular. After the success of his song, pop radio was more open to playing songs with rap. This album ended up having seven number-one singles, including the songs from the remix album that was released.

The single "My Prerogative" from that album is one of the songs most sung in karaoke and one of the most played songs on the radio. It's also used in a lot of spoofs and movies. As a matter of fact, basketball star Lebron James sang it, making a mockery of himself at the ESPN Espy Awards. Boy he jacked that song up. (Lebron, if you ever pick up this book, let me give you some advice: don't quit your day job!)

Britney Spears also attempted to remake "My Prerogative." "Everybody always asks me what I think about her version, and the only thing I can say is 'The check was good.' I'll just leave it at that," says Bobby.

New Edition also paved the way for many artists today, but they don't get the credit for it. They contributed a lot to where music is today. Before Mary J. Blige ever thought about blending hip-hop and R&B, New Edition had been incorporating rap into R&B songs. It really didn't get any attention until Bobby added rap to the songs on the *Don't Be Cruel* album. Even at that time, it was still kind of overlooked. Although New Edition were the originators of this fusion, Mary J. Blige would get the credit for it a few years later.

Awards, Accolades and Honor

The Music Mecca of the South

Bobby won his first major award with New Edition in 1987. They won their first American Music Award. Although he had previously left the group for his solo career, he was still a part of that winning album. Before that, New Edition never knew where they stood in the industry as a group. After four years in the business and all the hard work, they were finally rewarded.

Bobby also won a Grammy with the *Don't Be Cruel* album and an Oscar for his hit single "On My Own" on the *Ghostbusters* soundtrack. "I don't remember ever seeing the Oscar," he reflects. "I know winning awards of this magnitude is an honor, but I've never really been big on awards or award shows. I was the one in the group that was known for not showing up. I never really respected award shows. I didn't attend them unless I was performing. If they didn't want me to perform, I didn't feel like I had a reason to be there. I could care less about a nomination. I wanted to perform to show that I was worthy of winning. To be totally honest, I won a whole lot of awards, but I can't tell you what they are."

In addition to winning many awards, he was the second black male teenager to have a number-one single on the pop charts with "My Prerogative." Stevie Wonder was the first with his single "Fingertips Pt 2" years prior to his.

While being nominated and winning awards didn't carry any weight with him, starting his own record label, Triple B Records, and opening his studio, Bosstown Studio, were two of the biggest accomplishments of his life. His office and studio were in Atlanta, Georgia.

His attraction to Atlanta came from the time he went there in 1987 to work with Cameo, one of the hottest groups at the time. Atlanta Knights was the only hot nightclub in the city, and he fell in love with the vibe and the women. "Atlanta had some of the most beautiful black women that you ever wanted to see. I was like, 'This is my new home!'" Bobby exclaims.

Moving to Atlanta, his intentions were to blow it up and make it the big music capitol. I guess he succeeded because today Atlanta is known as the Black Hollywood, and referred to as the Music Mecca of the South. This movement drew other major black stars to Atlanta. Now Atlanta is one of the number-one cities where affluent blacks live.

There was also a lot of talent in Atlanta that he wanted to tap into. Not to mention, he thought Atlanta would be the safest and cheapest place to bring his family and set them up. A lot of his family was talented as well. He was grooming his nephews and sisters, getting them ready for the industry.

Under his record label, he signed his sister Carole, known as "Coupe B," who was a rapper; three R&B singers, his sister Lee Lee, Dee Dee O'Neal and Harold Travis; a rap act by the name of Stylz; and a duet called Smooth Sylk (Pia & KB). He released a compilation album with all of his artists called the B. Brown Posse, but for the most part, the label didn't get off the ground. He really didn't have the time to put into it.

Although his label never took off, just about every successful artist that came out of Atlanta recorded at his studio at some time or another. All of the major artists that came to town recorded at his studio also. Bosstown was almost like what Motown Hitsville U.S.A. was over forty years ago. All the big hits were coming out of his studio. From TLC to OutKast and every other artist that was making big records. All of the major producers that were making big records like Dallas Austin, Jermaine Dupri, and Teddy Riley also recorded at Bosstown.

He even recorded with some of the biggest athletes who were trying to make it in the music industry. On one occasion, Shaquille O'Neal flew to Atlanta so that Ralph and Bobby could work on his project with him in his studio. Shaq liked Bobby's sound and style and wanted to incorporate it into his music. Their chemistry was pretty good together.

Although Bosstown was the number-one place to record in the South, unfortunately Bobby began to lose his celebrity artists and producers. One of the main reasons the studio fell apart was because he got married, got sidetracked, and started living this whole other life, totally neglecting the business. The people that he left in charge to run the place could not maintain it. Eventually, he went out of business.

Now the studio is owned by OutKast, and it's called Stankonia. It's been years since Bobby's been there, but OutKast are keeping it up and have kept it pretty much the same way he left it, which means a lot to him because that place has a lot of history. He was even thinking about trying to work it out to turn it into a museum like what Motown Hitsville U.S.A. is today. This would be a great addition to the accolades he received in the city of Atlanta. Mayor Maynard Jackson awarded him a key to the city as well as a street named in his honor, Bobby Brown Parkway.

Chapter 5

A Magnet for Bad Luck

"The Rise and Fall"

Ain't Nobody Humpin' Around

Dirty Dancing

The first time Bobby ever had a run-in with the law was at one of his concerts. Before this, he never had a speeding ticket. He had been accused of what the media would term an "overly suggestive stage performance" and what the law called lewd conduct.

He had a dance move that he did where he would gyrate and pump his hips that drove the ladies crazy. After his shows the media wrote stories that the girls, their mothers, and their grandmothers all lost their minds during his performances and that they hadn't seen such sexual excitement on stage since the days of Sam Cooke and Jackie Wilson.

I think this particular dance offended the authorities and conservatives and got their women all hot and bothered. Therefore, they made it their business to make sure police were waiting on him in every city that he performed in to arrest him the minute he began to "pump." Well, they didn't actually arrest him. His management would just pay the fine after each show so that he didn't have to go to jail. But of course by the time media put it out, it was, "Bobby Brown goes down for lewd conduct."

He was the second person in the industry to ever get charged in the state of Georgia with lewd conduct. One of the entertainers Bobby has always looked up to, Elvis Presley, was the first. Ironically, they both had hit records called "Don't Be Cruel" and he was pretty good with the women as well.

Bobby had been gyrating and pumping his pelvis since New Edition, but it hit the fan when New Edition showed up at a concert in Washington, D.C., the capital. It was one of the last concerts he did with the group. He has a vivid recollection of this night. "I remember this show perfectly. We were performing in front of 1.5 million people. I remember the colors we wore and everything. We had on white pants, white shirts, and purple jackets. Before the show, the police made an announcement saying, 'There won't be no gyrating from Mr. Brown. We will not have that here.' I always rebelled against people taking shots at me. This only added fuel to my fire. I did it anyway!"

I think it was after the D.C. show that the authorities started focusing on his performances. Some cities wouldn't bother him, but others would. When some of these cities fined him, the fines were so small he didn't pay them any attention.

I guess after not getting any cooperation from him, they felt they were wasting their time, so they stopped harassing him altogether. He continued to do his dance throughout his career and still does it to this very day. These days the younger artists' performances are ten times more obscene than his dances were. I guess it took him and Elvis to go through the motions to open doors for the next generation.

Losing It All

Financial Woes

When he lost his studio, record label, and mansion, it was because he left them for other individuals to take care of after his marriage. He left his mother the mansion and other family members the studio and record label. He told them to take care of each other because he was living a different life with Whitney. He started assisting her with her career. In the process, everything that he built fell apart. It became apparent that his people could not hold the business together without him. He sat back and watched the empire that he built come tumbling down. Bobby expresses that, "It wasn't like I could just come in and try to save everything because, the way I looked at it, it would cost more than it was worth to try to salvage all three places."

He also had the IRS knocking at his door. They were saying that he owed them a couple of million dollars in back taxes. Everyone knows how Uncle Sam is when he wants his money. Bobby had to work that out before he could even think about doing anything else.

As far as his assets were concerned, he did not see it as losing everything. He was living a great life with Whitney. So you could say he lost all of his past possessions that he wasn't using anymore. He hated to see it go because it was still feeding his family, and there was a lot of sentimental value there. His life with his wife was a whole lot more fulfilling. The whole idea of starting this new and beautiful life with a wife and child had him overwhelmed.

While everybody was out saying Bobby is bankrupt and he is losing all of his possessions, he was off living in their mansion in New Jersey or one of their vacation homes in Hollywood, Florida, or one of the other places they owned real estate. He was married to one of the wealthiest women in the entertainment business. Realistically, how was he bankrupt?

Eventually, Whitney stepped in, and they made a deal on his mansion in Atlanta. The bank was trying to foreclose on it, and Whitney bailed him out. "I ended up doing a little trick where I sold the house to her and we ended up still being able to pull the equity out of the house," says Bobby. It's kind of like selling something of major value for a dollar in order to reap the benefits on the back end. If you didn't understand, it's only because you weren't supposed to. Remember it was a trick, and tricks aren't to be told.

After he got married his life took a turn for the best and the worst. I say for the best because he had a wife that he loved and a newborn child through his marriage. I say for the worst because he let his past life fall to the wayside. That meant losing everything he had in the past to gain his new life. Basically it boiled down to closing one chapter of his life and opening a new one.

Death All Around

Burying Family and Friends .

Bobby started experiencing people dying around him at a very young age. He thinks this kind of shaped his idea of what he feels about death and funerals to this very day. Bobby states, "I don't go to funerals or attend wakes because of my perception of death." When he lost his friend Jimmy at the age of ten, I think it scarred him for life. He explains, "I actually watched him get killed and felt bad because I couldn't save him." Jimmy was his best friend at the time, and they went through a lot together. On the day of his death they had been out riding stolen bikes with some other friends. They used to steal bikes because their families couldn't afford to buy them their own. They'd ride around the projects looking for things to get into. They pulled up at a party and decided to hang out for a while. "When we came out of the party there was a boy sitting on Jimmy's stolen bike," recalls Bobby. "Jimmy took offense and had a few words with the boy. One thing led to another, and before you know it, Jimmy brutally beat this boy down to the ground. Jimmy was in no way a pushover. He was a Golden Gloves boxer like me, and he knew martial arts. Jimmy was beating the boy so bad one of the boy's friends threw him a knife. Another friend of ours who was standing around saw the knife and panicked. He kicked the boy, trying to make him drop the knife, but instead the boy fell into Jimmy with the knife. He stabbed him straight in the heart."

Two weeks after Jimmy's death, Bobby's grandmother died. He was close to her, so he took this very hard. It was too much for him to deal with at one time. He was never the same again when it came to death. He doesn't know what happened to him psychologically, but these two deaths are the reason why he can't go to funerals.

A little over ten years later he found himself in the middle of another murder of someone close to him. One night in 1995 he made headline news and had his first brush with death. That might have been the luckiest night of his life. To this very day, he still doesn't understand how he's still here. He knew then that God had plans for him.

He had gone back home to Boston to visit his children, La Princia and Lil Bobby. He drove up there from the mansion he and Whitney owned in New Jersey. He was riding in his new Bentley that Whitney had given him. Whitney had received it as a gift from the producers of the movie *Bodyguard*. She gave it to Bobby because he was the person who negotiated the contracts for the movie and soundtrack. At the time, he and Whitney were having a few marital problems, so he decided to get out of town to gather his thoughts and visit his children. Upset and distraught, he started on his journey, stopping off in New York to party with Dennis Rodman at the China Club. Bobby expresses, "Dennis and I got wasted. We had a drinking contest with shots of tequila. I tried to drink my problems away that night. I got so drunk that I don't know how I made it to Boston. However, and whatever angel got me there, I was blessed to get there. Early the next morning, I woke up with my car parked on Kim's lawn, La Princia and Lil Bobby's mother."

Upon arriving in Boston, he didn't know he would be in for the shock of his life. After seeing his children and recovering from his hangover, he went out with his sister Carole's fiancé, Seally. Seally had a reputation for being a tough guy around town. He was involved with some of the local gangs, which should've been a red flag for him. Bobby reflects, "But since Bobby had the Big Willie, 'I'm not scared of nothing' type attitude, I threw myself right in the middle of a rivalry.'"

They went to the club where the gangs usually hang. Bobby knew members of both gangs. Using his status, he started buying drinks for everybody, trying to bring everyone together. He called himself trying to settle a beef that had been going on between two of the gangs. In the process of doing this, tempers between several of the guys started to flare. So he decided to leave the scene since things were getting heated. While getting in the car, Seally handed him a gun and told him there was about to be some trouble so cover himself. Before Bobby could crank the car a guy ran over to Seally's side and shot him in the head a couple of times. Then two other guys ran up to his side of the car and started unloading machine guns. "Imagine rounds of bullets being shot into a car while you're sitting in it," says Bobby. "All I could do was get into the floorboard of the vehicle. I actually curled up and folded my entire body in that little area of the car where the pedals are. Now I'm a strong believer that a person can do anything when he's put into a life or death situation."

He continues, "Looking back at the guys shooting, I could actually see the bullets coming at me. I felt like I was in the movie, "The Matrix." Every time a bullet came toward me, I would miraculously move my body to dodge the bullet. There were so many bullets coming at me, I felt like they were actually bouncing off of me. There was no way I was supposed to escape getting hit. Finally, the shooting stopped, and I could hear the guns clicking as the shooters continued pulling the triggers. I immediately thought, 'He must be out of bullets!' My first instinct was to push open the car door to escape. As I attempted to get out, another car pulled up on my side of the car and started shooting again. I quickly ducked back in, but this time I took the gun I had in my hand and started shooting back. I was able to shoot my way out of the car. I ran across the street and immediately tossed the gun. By this time, I saw some cops running toward me. They started shouting, 'It's you! You're shooting, huh.' I started explaining to them the situation the best I could. My mind was more focused on getting back to the car so we could get SEally to the hospital." When they got over to the car, Sealy was still holding on for his life. He had two shots in his head, and his body was tore up from multiple gunshot wounds. There were 178 bullets in Bobby's brand new Bentley. It had to be a miracle for him to walk away with a bullet graze. Sealy wasn't so lucky. He died by the time they arrived at the hospital. This incident made headline news all over the world. Bobby had escaped death and lost another person close to him.

Bobby had a nervous breakdown after this. He was covered in so much blood that night he didn't know whether he was dead or alive. This incident sent him straight to the Betty Ford Alcohol and Drug Treatment Center. "I started drinking uncontrollably, and I was smoking more weed than a Rastafarian," remembers Bobby. "I became a weed head. On top of all that, Whitney's and my marital problems didn't help the situation. My head was already screwed up. Then to find myself in the middle of a shootout."

Some years later, once again he was faced with the death that devastated him the most. His oldest sister Bethy died of lung cancer. This tore him up. Bethy was the strength of their family. She was always the one that kept order in the family. When there were disputes, she always stepped in and put the fire out. She was the backbone of all his siblings.

Bethy had a last request when she found out she was dying. She asked that they would take her to Jerusalem, the Promised Land. Bobby and Whitney obliged, and this is what sparked their famous trip to the Promised Land. At the time, Whitney was working on a Christmas album, so to be in the Holy land was definitely an inspiration for the project.

Bobby and his family met with the Prime Minister and everyone treated them like royalty. They toured the Old Christian city of Jerusalem and visited the Galilee and Jordan Rivers. After taking in some massages at a resort, they decided to have a little fun. Early in the day they parasailed over the Red Sea and later took a cruise on this spiritual sea that was parted by Moses in the Bible. Bethy loved every minute of it, and it was a dream come true for her. This made Bobby's heart feel good!

"Seeing her face light up and the calmness that came over her from the fact that she knew she was on sacred land definitely let us all know she was going to be alright," says Bobby. She died not long after the trip. Although the family lost an angel, Bobby thinks they all had braced themselves and were prepared for her departure. Although he didn't usually attend funerals, the death of Bethy was an exception to the rule. He would not have missed her home going for anything in the world. Bethy was so loved, they had to have services in Atlanta and Boston. Each funeral was filled to capacity because Bethy had touched the hearts of so many.

Chapter 6

Whitney Houston

"The Untold Truth"

Living as a Power Couple

Love Endures

Bobby met Whitney at the Soul Train Music Awards in 1989. She was sitting behind him during the show. "All of a sudden, I felt someone poking me in the back of my head," Bobby says. "Startled, I turned around like, 'Who in the——?What the——!' It was Whitney Houston. She said, 'Excuse me, was I hitting you?' I said, 'Yeah, you were hitting me, but it's okay as long as it was you.' At that moment, I thought, 'She's flirting with me.' I knew it was my chance to move in, so I went for the jugular. I said to her, 'If I asked you to go on a date would you say yes?' She was like, 'Yea!'" Not long after, they went on their first date. They hooked up in L.A. and went shopping on Rodeo Drive. Right away they hit it off. She was nothing like her TV persona. He was under the impression that she was this prim and proper, conservative chick that he would have to break in. That was the furthest thing from the truth. She was so down to earth! They had a great time!

They are both romantics at heart, so there was a lot of cuddling and smooching. It was that immediate chemistry—you know, that connection where you can see yourself spending valuable time with someone or maybe even your life.

For their next few dates they went to eat at a couple of restaurants, the typical friendly things. After that, they didn't see each other for a while because their schedules were too hectic. However, they talked on the phone a few times.

A couple of months later, she invited him to her birthday party at her mansion in New Jersey. When he got the news from his staff, "I was like, 'Ohhhh, yeah, she wants me,'" says Bobby. The way she invited him was very cordial. She kept it professional. Her assistant sent an invitation to his manager. Of course, he accepted.

On the day of the party, he flew into Jersey. He got all decked out in a silk outfit, laid the hair down, and got his Gumby all tight. He totally prepped himself for the occasion. The Gumby hairdo was his specialty! (For those of you who don't know what the Gumby is, it was a high-right, low-left fade that was invented by a cartoon character named Gumby. However, Bobby was responsible for making it popular in the urban culture.) After he started rockin' the Gumby, it became a famous style for the entire black community.

Bobby arrived at Whitney's mansion with his buddy Donnie Simpson, the host of BET's video show where he had confessed his love for Janet Jackson early on in his career and scored. (I guess Donnie must be some kind of good luck charm for him.) When they walked into the foyer of her mansion, all he could say was, "Wow!" This chick was living larger than the president. At that point in his career he had been exposed to a lot of extravagant things, but to see her living like she was really impressed him.

They really connected at the party. She gave him a lot of special attention and made it clear to him that she wanted to see him again. They had a few drinks together, and she made it her business to introduce him to a couple of her friends. One thing I do know is when a woman introduces you to her family and friends you're definitely making progress. As they got to know one another, they realized they were just alike. They had so much in common that they became best friends. They both liked to have fun and enjoyed doing a lot of the same things like watching movies on DVD, trying new restaurants, shopping, and spending quality time with their families. When he was with Whitney it seemed like the whole world stopped and they were the only ones that existed.

At the time, Whitney was on the road a lot. He'd meet her in different cities at her shows. When she wasn't on the road, she'd visit him at his home in Atlanta. Most of the time, they stayed in hotels because she didn't like to stay at his haunted mansion. She used to hear strange noises in the middle of the night. She said that his house was one of the spookiest places she had ever been.

Their relationship started to take off. They went on romantic vacations to private islands around the world. They took cruises on private yachts. Every free moment they had, they spent it together. Everything was happening at a fast pace. Everyone started voicing their opinions. People were trying to figure out how they were together. They seemed like such an odd couple, Whitney being the All-American girl-next-door figure and Bobby being looked at as more of a bad boy. What people didn't know was that Whitney had an edge. The worlds they came from were pretty much the same. Her record label just did a great job of painting a different picture through her music.

Besides their physical chemistry, they also had bedroom chemistry. "I've always been known to be a pretty good lover," says Bobby. "The word on the street is that I'm well-endowed."

Ignoring all the critics like they always have, before he knew it, they rushed off to the altar. In the summer of 1992 the whole world watched as the Princess of Pop and the Bad Boy tied the knot. Their wedding was described as being one of the most star-studded weddings of all time. Princes and princesses from other countries and the biggest celebrities in the world were there. Donald Trump, Clive Davis, Dionne Warwick, Patti Labelle, Dick Clark, Gloria Estefan, Gladys Knight, and a list of others all showed up at their mansion in New Jersey. The wedding took place in a very extravagant tent on their property. There were expensive champagnes flowing from every fountain, and some of their favorite artists performed at the reception. It was one of the greatest days of his life. Boy, if only they had known what was to come!

After getting married they recorded a song together for Bobby's third album, *Bobby*, called "We Have Something in Common," and it established them as a power couple in the industry. It was one of the biggest duets by a couple since Sonny and Cher. Bobby had just come off the success of the *Don't Be Cruel* album, and Whitney, of course, was Whitney!

Bobby explains, "Going into the studio with Whitney was somewhat intimidating. She is such a great singer that it was hard for me to sing with her. She had so much of an effect on me in the studio that I would get butterflies in my stomach when I worked with her. I am certain I'm not the only one that this has happened to. With such an amazing voice, she had that affect on everyone."

As their relationship grew, the more everyone tried to come between them—the media, some of the people around them, and anyone that had nothing else to do with their time but worry about their business.

Bobby thinks it was the fact that he and Whitney had such a strong relationship with God that gave them stability and made them the power couple that they were. Their love was Godly. Miraculously, they both have the same birthmark in two places. To them, this was a symbol that signified they were meant to be together.

Being with her made him tap into feelings that he had never been in touch with. Most of the slow songs he wrote were inspired by her. "I was so in love with her that I would just put my heart in a song, which is why all of my songs came out very emotional," says Bobby.

In the beginning, another part of their relationship was about family. They were all about bringing their relatives together. They would host family reunions for both of their families whenever they had the time. They always did things like this when they had down time. "It was always good to see everyone in one place at one time, especially since it wasn't that often that we got to see everyone because of our hectic schedules," remembers Bobby.

As time progressed they learned more about each other and went through their ups and downs, trials and tribulations. But it was their undying love that kept them together. They became a power couple in the public eye, and everyone wanted to hear and know more about them.

Life Under the Microscope

Privacy Please

The fact that Bobby and Whitney were together put them under a microscope. The marriage of two of the biggest stars in the business was definitely fodder for tabloids. All of a sudden the media wanted to know his every move—Who else was he seeing? What else was he doing? Did he drink too much or smoke too much? Did he drive his cars too fast?—basically any of his extracurricular activities.

Before this, the media hardly ever bothered him. He was small news. However, when he hooked up with Whitney Houston, he turned into the "biggest thing since John Wayne!" They were the hottest topic all over the world! People were waiting on the next story from the Bobby Brown, Whitney Houston saga. Their celebrity became more about their personal lives than their music careers.

This is why their reality show broke all kinds of records when they released it. Everybody in the world tuned in to see exactly what was going on in their lives. People wanted to see what all the fuss was about. Evidently, they got an eyeful because every week the ratings got better and better. I guess he and Whitney were everything they made them out to be. He was silly, and Whitney was silly, another side of her the public wasn't used to seeing. It made great TV, which is why millions of households tuned in each week to find out what would happen next.

Now Whitney blames the show for ruining her career, and she won't sign off on the contract to release the DVD. "I have a serious problem with this because this affects my income," says Bobby. "There is a lot of money to be made off the DVD, but because she won't cooperate, we'll never see it. First of all, I never asked her to show up on one of the sets. She would take it upon herself to show up anyway. I even went as far as telling her that she could leave. I made sure she knew she did NOT have to be there, but she always found a way to end up on the set. Now she regrets being a part of it."

Doing his reality show was like therapy for him. He learned a lot about himself and about his marriage. It was definitely marriage counseling for he and Whitney. "When we watched the show together, we were able to see our good and bad points," states Bobby. "We'd talk about them and try to work them out. I'd make comments to her about how she tried to handle me on the show, and she would comment on my behavior." The one thing in particular that they always had words about was how friendly he was to fans. Whitney always had a problem with this, especially when it came to the women. She considered his interactions with female fans flirting. Bobby explains, "Whitney is the type that doesn't like to be disturbed when she's out in public, but it doesn't bother me at all. I'm a people person."

Once your personal life starts to play out in public, it's kind of hard for a lot of people to continue to respect your craft. Whether you are a musician or actor, people start losing focus on what made you who you are in the first place. This is really sad. There are a lot of great entertainers out there that have had their careers overshadowed by the tabloids, and Bobby and Whitney are in that number.

A lot of people like to start rumors and make false accusations. "My philosophy has always been 'Don't judge a book by its cover,' meaning don't judge a man to be wrong until you get to know him," Bobby expresses. "If you see or hear something about me, don't judge me until you get a chance to hear it from me."

Sometimes it gets so crazy he can't even go in a restaurant and eat without it making headlines. Bobby reflects, "I remember on one occasion I was in the World Pie restaurant in Miami with some friends having dinner, and the next day it was in the papers. 'Bobby Brown was in the restaurant flirting with the hostess.' It was ridiculous. Major headlines!" First of all, anyone that knows Bobby knows that he's a very friendly person. He could just carry on a conversation with any stranger at any given time. Tabloids would just take things out of context over a simple conversation.

This was one of the reasons why he and Whitney ignored tabloids and the other media. If Whitney had listened to half of the things that people said, they would have been divorced a long time ago. It was like the more they ignored them, the stranger the accusations became. There were stories of how he ate, how his jaws were moving. "I mean, give me a break! Every now and then I would read this stuff just to get a laugh," Bobby explains.

The most current story is definitely one of the wildest ones of all time. Just the other day Bobby went to the doctor to get a checkup because he was having chest pains, which turned out to be gas that had built up in his chest. Within hours the whole story was twisted. It was major news around the country that he was rushed to the hospital because he had a mild heart attack.

Another ridiculous rumor was that he was dying and one of his family members had a tape of him saying his good-byes to his loved ones. The tape was supposedly being sold for $100,000. This incident was a misunderstanding about some old footage that he and a friend had recorded in the past for a show, not a deathbed confession. He had to go on national TV to clear up many rumors.

Due to the paparazzi and these media scandals, he and Whitney would check into hotels under aliases. Most of the time, they went by the name of Justin Case. They came up with this under the presumption of just in case they need to be contacted. After a while they had to change names because the paparazzi always had a way of finding out what their alias was.

Bobby understands the whole concept of the media using he and Whitney as bait to catch more readers for their publications. The media found out that whenever they ran a story on them their sales would increase. It was business for them. For Bobby, personally, he could've cared less about what they wrote. At the end of the day, they had to go on with their lives and raise their family.

Bobby and Whitney had their arguments and fights just like everyone else. It wasn't no Ike and Tina type of fights, but that's what the media made the public believe. "I mean, I'm guilty of getting upset and flying off the handle a little. I was known to throw a bottle or two at a wall or something. Things that I'd regret later, I would be responsible for cleaning up or having the wall repaired. What people fail to realize is that Whitney is no punk. She definitely knows how to handle and defend herself in situations that could have potentially been violent. Some of the stories in the media made me out to be like Ike Turner, when that wasn't my character," Bobby explains.

There was one story in particular that he feels the media did a great job of blowing out of proportion. It was the incident where he smacked Whitney. They used to horseplay a lot, and on this day he smacked her kind of hard and ran out the house laughing. She got upset and called the police because she was startled and offended, although she knew he didn't mean any harm. He was on his way out of town, so he headed to the airport. When he got news that she called the police, he went back home to apologize. By this time, the police were already looking for him with a warrant for domestic violence. When the media found out, they turned it into a circus.

Bobby and Whitney went through a lot in their marriage. Through all the things they endured, it took a strong couple to stick together. "We came up with our own personal word to describe our relationship, *stickability*," says Bobby. This word represents what they stood for during those trying times. It pretty much meant that they had the capability of winning if they could stick in there and beat whatever the odds were against them.

Sometimes the odds were so strong it was almost like fighting against the tides. Especially in their position, they were up against the whole world. Their whole personal life was on a stage for people to take shots at them. "When your family, friends, and all of the people around you start going against you, then that really stacks the deck," says Bobby.

It was always their love that kept them together. A lot of things in their relationship, they just ran with in the name of love. You have to realize that love is a win-lose situation. When you choose love, you are always going to have your good times and bad. There are a lot of great points about love, but there is always something that can go wrong. There is always something that can hurt or harm you. There is always the possibility of losing, but you have to stick in there and make the best of it.

Their biggest inspirations during trying times were Ossie Davis and his wife. They were a true testament of how to be a black celebrity couple. They were a true depiction of how to weather all of the storms by balancing your career and love life. They were both actors that survived in this industry as a power couple for fifty years. Or shall I say, 'til death do us part. When Ossie died a few years ago, it was devastating to a lot of people who looked up to him.

They also turned to Bill and Camille Cosby. Bobby and Whitney looked at their lives and what they went through and tried to make adjustments in their lives based on Bill and Camille's success. They dealt with extramarital affairs and pretty much everything else you can go through in a public relationship. They stayed together through it all. Bobby knows from experience that it's hard to go through those types of situations, especially when it's being played out in front of the world.

Losing My Identity

From Bobby Brown to Bobby Houston

After he started dating Whitney, the word around the industry was that he was lovesick because he slowed down on a lot of his business activities. It didn't help that it took two and a half years for him to come back with his next album, Bobby. Everybody made a big deal out of it. He had found the love of his life. But on another note, he was also taking a break from all of the success he had with the Don't Be Cruel album. "That album took me on the ride of my life!" exclaims Bobby.

Bobby had a lot of love and respect for Whitney. There wasn't anything in the world that he wouldn't have done for that woman. So he set aside a lot of his business, and he had become her sidekick, especially after they were married. He had started to handle all of her business. He would do things like handle her tour management, assist with booking her movie roles, handle her music business, and even when she was on tour he'd just be there with her, watching their child. Whatever it took to make it work.

Bobby was perfectly fine with what he was doing. He had been working all his life. Now, he had a chance to take a break and be on the road with his family. He didn't need for money. He didn't need for anything. He let all of his business associates, friends, and relatives know that he was going to take some years off to be with his family. He made it clear to everyone that his family had become his number-one priority.

His personal life started taking a downward spiral after that. He stopped paying attention to almost everything he was involved in. He started refusing to do shows or go on tours and also declining movie roles. Being married had really become a big distraction for him. Looking back, although he made his own personal decision to assist Whitney, she played a very big part in him not working. She didn't like the idea of him leaving to work for long periods. She always wanted him with her, so he obliged.

Bobby pretty much devoted all his time to being a husband, assistant, and father. When he was off the scene people thought that he was just living off of Whitney, when in actuality he was behind the scenes helping with her career.

This is when the whole talk started about Whitney being the provider and him freeloading. It didn't help that her career was really taking off and she had been accepted by all cultures. She had become the token black woman, and he was her shadow. This became a joke to them because Whitney always had this thing where she thought she was more white than black. "I believe she got this idea from her being accepted in the industry by the white culture," says Bobby. "I never understood how she felt like this when I knew she was more 'Negro' than I am. Not African-American, but more 'Negro' than I could ever be. That is one of the reasons why I always loved her so much, because she was so real!"

The movie *Bodyguard* had a lot to do with Whitney's total acceptance in the white culture. She was already a crossover artist from her music, but it went to another level after this movie. She was an African-American pop star playing alongside Kevin

Costner, one of the most powerful white actors in the industry. Not to mention that the soundtrack from the movie is still one of the biggest selling soundtracks in history. Whitney had the lead single on this album. She took an old country song recorded by Dolly Parton called "I Will Always Love You" and made it one of the biggest songs in the world, and I do mean the entire world! Whitney's version of this song sent sales through the roof, making it one of the highest-selling soundtracks of all time. The *Bodyguard* movie and soundtrack took her over the top and made her larger than life, transcending all cultures.

After this success, the media definitely made it their business to address him as Mr. Whitney Houston or Mr. Bobby Houston. Not to say that he was offended or anything. "It's actually a pleasure to be known as marrying one of the most successful women in show biz. Life is too short to take offense to things like that," says Bobby. However, at the same time, he is his own man. He is very confident in himself. He never doubts who he is. He knows for a fact that he established a name for himself in the business as his own force. It just so happens Whitney was in a 747 and he was in a 727. She had the bigger plane; he's man enough to accept that. He has no problem with a woman having her own. His love for her was so strong it never got to a point where he felt like they had to compete or be in competition. It was more about them working together. It was about them building a foundation together. The fact that she had the bigger name or brought home the bigger check was never a big deal to him. Of course, the media tried to make him feel bad. What man wouldn't have loved to be in his position? I'm sure Steadman Graham, Oprah's significant other, would not mind being called Steadman Winfrey. She's a great woman of wealth and power that's been good to him, so what's the problem?

To set the record straight, "We were a team, a family working toward one goal," says Bobby. "Although Whitney made her share of financial decisions, I made a lot of financial decisions in our marriage on a personal and business level as well. When it came to business, I made sure she got the best deals possible. When she worked on her albums, I kept all her recording costs to a minimum. I did production on some of her albums without getting credit for it. I did anything to save money and keep overhead down. When it came to her movies, I made sure all of her contracts were intact and things of that nature."

All in all, Bobby doesn't see it being a bad thing to lose his identity to someone that Osama Bin Laden is in love with and wanted to make one of his wives. This shows the power and impact Whitney has had on the entire world. It was a rumor that he was on the Taliban's hit list for being her husband. "For a minute I feared for my life," says Bobby. "The most wanted man in the world wanted me dead; that's insane!"

Chapter 7

All about Family

"Bobby Loves the Kids"

No Matter What

Blood Is Thicker than Water

Bobby has always said that the proudest moments in his life were being present to see his kids arrive into this world. Nothing means more to him in life than the birth of his children. He could care less about any type of award, or anything else for that matter. Nothing will ever replace these precious moments.

Children are a gift from God. They are replicas of their parents. They might have their mother's hair, their father's lips, mother's eyes, father's walk, and so on. I think this is a unique phenomenon and a blessing to see parts of yourself reflected to you from another human being.

I am also amazed by the natural, unconditional love between the parent and child. No matter what happens or how long you are apart from a child, there is always going to be an automatic emotional bond on some level.

Bobby's oldest son, Landon, is now twenty-four.

He had him right after he left New Edition. Bobby speaks candidly about their relationship. "Landon and I have our fights, misunderstandings, and battles. But he knows that I love him dearly. I think that's just the process of a young man coming into manhood. It's inevitable; a growing boy is going to challenge his parents for some of the things that he believes in. I have no problem with this; I went through the same thing. And since he is my first son, I need him to succeed probably more than any other man in my life."

Landon is on a new reality show on MTV called *Rock the Cradle*. It's a singing competition between the children of different rock stars to see who has what it takes to step out of their parents' shadow. Bobby explains, "Landon definitely has what it takes to compete with the best of them. Watching him grow up and pursue his dreams makes me proud. I know he always wanted to be an entertainer, so it feels good to see him become the man he has always wanted to be."

He continues, "My youngest son, Lil Bobby—I wear his name tattooed proudly on my arm. He's just like me! I don't worry about him; I know whatever he chooses to do in life he's going to succeed. I don't know whether it's going to be in the entertainment business, but whatever he does, he is going to achieve. Me personally, I think he should pursue a singing career because he sings like a bird."

"All of my kids are basically entertainers. I guess it's just in their blood. However, one of them has other dreams and aspirations than following in my footsteps. My oldest daughter, La Princia, wants to be a lawyer or an accountant. She feels these are the two professionals that I need in order for me to survive in this world. I'm very proud of her. She is a very compassionate and ambitious person. Now that she has entered college, she can pursue her dreams of helping me in this cold, cold world that is trying to suck me up!"

"Whitney may have given birth to my baby girl, Bobbi Kristina, but she is my spitting image. She has my personality and all. You know when two people have the same characteristics they clash at times. Whitney has always told me that I met my match when Bobbi Kris came into the world. Although Lil Bobby and Brandon both have amazing voices, I think Bobbi Kris is going to blow the whole world away. She has everything it takes to be a great entertainer. She has her mother's voice and my legs; she's a dancing machine. That's a great combination. If she uses both of her God-given talents, she is going to make a major impact on the world."

"My kids made me grow up," he confesses. "They made me realize that I can't play around forever. They gave me a sense of responsibility. Landon, La Princia, Lil Bobby, and Bobbi Kris mean EVERYTHING to me, and I would give them the world if I could. I have a great relationship with all of them, and I constantly work to strengthen and make each one grow."

Living as One

The Family

They were all one big happy family. Every chance Bobby got, he made sure all of his kids were around him. Whenever he got free time, he and Whitney flew his kids to wherever they were in the world. They paraded around the country as one. Whether they were at Disney World or at their Hollywood beach house, they always found time to spend together.

It was very important for him to keep all of his children together. Although they have three different mothers and live in different parts of the country, they are all very close and love one another as if they are one family under one roof.

He always made sure that he spent as much time as possible with his kids to make sure they were well grounded. Growing up with parents that are in the limelight can definitely be a distraction for kids. So he always made it his business to explain to them that this was their job and tried to keep them away from the spotlight as much as possible.

The media never really affected he and Whitney. Most of the time they laughed at some of the accusations. However, the one way the media could affect him was when they talked about his kids. Anything they said about his kids bothered him far more than anything they said about him. His kids are his babies. They are what he lives for. They don't have anything to do with his downfalls. They are innocent. If you want to rub him the wrong way, just talk about his kids. The media used to say some very offensive things. They talked about how he had illegitimate kids because he fathered children outside of marriage. They would take a shot with anything they could dig up. Sometimes he contemplated personally addressing some of these reporters when they made these statements. This is just the natural instinct of a father and protector. But it was always the better side of him that made him turn the other cheek.

He and his kids express their love for one another in different ways. They are very overprotective of Bobby, as he is of them. They are well aware of the things that he has to go through with the media. They have to go through them as well because every time a new story develops about him everyone looks at them, too. In the past, when it came to Bobby, they were very sensitive toward others that criticized or made fun of him. Over the years, they have learned to develop thick skin, let it bounce off, and remain strong during these crises.

Bobby loves kids in general. What people don't know is he practically raised some of his nieces and nephews. He is close to all of them. They all pretty much had rooms in all of his homes. It was like they were all his children. They stayed with him whenever they wanted.

It feels good to know that he has formed a bond with his kids that is beyond words. He successfully raised a family that is so far away but yet so close at heart. When you have love, there is no distance that can come between you. He instilled this in them and made them realize that, although they are not together all the time, blood is thicker than water.

Things Change

Income Bracket

It came to a point that Bobby stopped making the kind of money that he had been when he was mandated to pay child support. He wasn't able to make those large payments as completely and promptly as he had in the past. What people don't know is that his kids have always been taken care of. Early in his career, all of his royalties from album sales went to his daughter La Princia. He had it set up this way so he wouldn't have to worry about her future. He would live day to day off of his tour money and earnings from the merchandise sales at his concert, and the royalties were set aside for her. As he continued to have more kids, he split the royalties between them equally.

Bobby has always boasted that all three of his four kid's mothers are great (Malika, Kim, and Whitney). They are all caregivers and very hands-on with his kids. Although La Princia's and Bobby's mother, Kim, takes him to court for child support every now and then, he doesn't have anything against her. She's been a wonderful mother to his kids. He doesn't have a problem with the whole child-support issue. He does the best he can. He doesn't make the kind of money that he used to, so a lot of times it's a little challenging to make those same payments that he made when the money was flowing more freely. For the most part, whenever he was arrested, he paid it all in full. Once he had to pay up to $60,000 before he was released and another time, $20,000. It wasn't like he was neglecting his kids; they had whatever they wanted, and their mother just wanted her due.

At one time, he and Whitney had an account that all of the bills were automatically paid from, so everyone received their checks on time. He doesn't know how or when that account stopped, but all of a sudden, everyone was saying he owed them money.

When he had to take the responsibility of paying the bills himself, most of the time he got so caught up in his business that time would pass him by, and before he knew it, he was months behind. He was never really good at these types of things. Lack of communication definitely played a part also in his getting behind.

The crazy part is that they always found a fine time to arrest him on these child-support charges. Twice they arrested him while he was watching his daughter La Princia in cheerleading competitions. One of the times he had just left the concession stand, and he sat down to eat. He had literally just bought a hot dog and chips when the boys in blue approached him. When they said, "Mr. Brown, you're gonna have to come with us," he just stood up and assumed the position. It was like he had become the mascot with the handcuffs. He'd just show up in Boston and go to the competition, unaware of the warrants. The next thing you know, he's in cuffs.

I believe we as men have to take responsibility for our kids. If we can lie down and help make them, we should be ready and willing to help raise them. Unfortunately, he has not been there for his kids every step of the way due to the nature of his business and hectic schedule, but he tries to make it up to them every chance he gets.

His daughter La Princia is in college now, so he's just left to pay Lil Bobby's support, which is more manageable. Bobby explains, "The bottom line is, I'm going to always be there for my kids, no matter how old they get. They can always call up Daddy, and I'm there!"

Chapter 8

The Reigning King . . .

"My Perception"

The State of R&B

Speak Out

Bobby never said he was the King of R&B. That was something that Whitney said. She went on national TV at a BET event and said he was the King of R&B. From that point on, everybody made a big deal out of it. "That title was never something that I claimed," he reveals. "I always looked at myself as a performer. As I mentioned earlier, I've always considered myself the King of Stage. To this very day, I still don't think anyone can get with me on the stage. I own the stage. I'm a true performer at heart. Although I like making the money, I like performing more. I love the energy that the crowd gives me. I draw from the crowd. It's really like nothing else, no other feeling. It's like the birth of a child."

A lot of the young guys in R&B now remind him of himself. "Usher and Omarion definitely have a lot of my flavor," he claims. "I call them little mini me's! I can tell that they love performing. I watched one of Usher's shows, and he basically did my whole show. It was as if it was me on stage. The thing about it is, I love seeing that. It's a compliment to me as a performer, and I'd like to thank them all."

I think artists take bits and pieces of craft from other artists that came before them. As for Bobby, when he went solo, he would emulate parts of Prince, Michael Jackson, or James Brown. I think you take parts of whoever is the hottest act of that era and you incorporate that into your own style. It's just like taking buttermilk, eggs, and cornmeal; you whip it up, bake it, and you have cornbread. It's mixing different ingredients into one to come out with a different hot product.

"Out of all the R&B artists out there today, I am most proud of Usher," says Bobby. "I don't have a problem with him emulating my style. I personally trained him once. I am aware of the fact that he gives me some credit for inspiring him, just like I give the ones that came before me their due credit. It's the way of the business. You have to pay respect to those who helped you become who you are."

At this point in time the state of R&B has been watered down. It's a digitalized world. You don't see the use of real instruments in music anymore. I want the old R&B back. Real R&B is a blend of rhythm and blues like Earth Wind & Fire and Barry White. Motown started the sound back in the sixties, and artists like Al Green and Betty Wright gave it a bluesier sound going into the seventies. It was originally designed by record companies to give the black music culture an identity for direct marketing. This created an avenue for advertisers to reach the black consumer through urban radio. It grew to be the giant that it is today and blended different styles.

Real R&B to me is soul music. Music you can feel deep down in your soul. When the artist on the mic is "saangin" (not singing, but "saangin"—there is a difference) it comes straight from their heart. It's like you're pouring your soul out. Whatever it is that you're going through or have been through comes out. It's pure emotion that makes the listener want to cry. Aretha Franklin "saangs," Luther Vandross "saangs," and of course, Whitney "saangs!" Back in the day, the hit makers were true singers. However, most of the music today has been watered down. R&B has lost its soul. It's more about the entertainment and dancing than it is about "saangin!"

Bobby's first album was R&B, but the *Don't Be Cruel* album was considered R&B/pop because of the New Jack Swing sound that was added to it. Through the decades, R&B has gone through many phases. We've had R&B/Funk, R&B/Pop, Hip-Hop/R&B, Crunk/R&B, and the latest, Neo Soul. Today, anything goes. R&B always has and always will revolutionize its sound and impact the music industry as a whole.

New Edition Reunion

The Divo Tour

W hen the idea was brought to Bobby about doing a New Edition reunion album, he didn't know what to think or expect. The idea had been tossed around for a few years before the project developed. He knew that it was always in the back of all of their minds to come back and do something together. It was only a matter of time. But to carry it out, they knew it was gonna take some work. First of all they were all waiting on their second solo albums to come out. They also knew they had to get over the politics of the business and overcome their conflicting schedules. Just think, six divos together who already had other things going on individually would inevitably be somebody's headache. I used the word divo because it is the male version of a diva, which I think they all were by the time of this project. But for the most part it all turned out well. They all came together as one. The album was created by each and every person in the group. They all had a lot of input on the record, and they all brought their own flavor to it. There were a lot of meetings and conference calls about how they were going to do things. It was a group effort.

At times it was a little stressful. Putting in the long hours would get everyone a little agitated. Everybody had times when they were having a bad day. Sometimes it could be something really small, but you would blow it out of proportion because it was your turn. They would have little arguments and keep it moving.

Once the album was all done, they called it *Home Again,* which was the title of one of the songs on the album. That title worked for all of them because they all felt that as individual acts New Edition was their home.

It was very surprising to see all of us work together in harmony at this stage in our careers. They still had chemistry. New Edition's coming back together was very big for the industry. They had all gone their separate ways and obtained solo success. It was a major event to come back together and put their egos aside to make another album. The proof was on the charts. In their first week of sales, all the old and new fans turned out to give them their first number-one album on the pop charts as a group.

Another reason why Bobby knew this reunion had to happen was that he didn't believe New Edition was where they needed to be in history. They needed to come back and put their stamp on history as a group. They were always underrated and never given the credit due when it came to some of the things they established in the music industry. When people were asking groups who they looked up to, New Edition was never on their list, or if it was it was one of the last. That was not good. They had worked too hard to receive no acknowledgement. When they resurfaced he believes their comeback put the final stamp on things.

As far as history is concerned, there hadn't been a young black teen group since the Jackson 5. The Jackson 5 came in and set the stage. It was New Edition that came in years later and set the trend that still exists. They were the second black teen group that opened the doors for all the other young groups that followed them, the ones who didn't know who the

Jackson 5 were. They even crossed over into the white pop world. Back when New Edition came out, industry executives weren't really checking for young new acts. The deck was stacked against them from the beginning. They were five young black guys from the projects trying to make it in this industry. It was definitely a challenge. A lot of doors had to be opened. Once again, he doesn't think they got the credit they deserved. He thinks it's going to take a movie on their life story for people to understand the significance of New Edition.

Back then, the guy who discovered them, Maurice Starr, had a vision. He came in and bogarted his way into the industry, which started the boy-band craze. When they left him, he started the group New Kids on the Block, who also had major success. This craze went into the nineties with other five-boy groups like Troop, Silk, Hi Five, N Sync, Backstreet Boys, and many more.

Coming back together again after all those years and having a number-one album on the charts definitely set the pace for a big tour. Their fans had been waiting for them to come back on the road. And come back they did! Their tour kicked off in December of 1996 in their hometown, Boston, at the Dorchester Centrum Center. Their opening act on the tour was Blackstreet, and in certain cities Keith Sweat and Michael Bivins' female group, 702. City after city, they showed up and gave the crowd what they had been missing, an energetic show. Walking through the tunnels of the arena, heading to the stage with the guys he started with brought back many memories. It had been years since they had performed at an arena together. You could hear and feel the excitement of the fans roaring as they knew they were about to take the stage. The closer they got, the louder the crowd got. Finally every light in the arena went off, and they positioned themselves on stage. It felt like old times. The crowd lost their minds. It was in the air; they were back and stronger than ever.

During the tour there were squabbles between group members but nothing more than what you would have with a sibling. You know how you might argue with your little brother because you wanted to watch one thing on TV and he wanted to watch something else. It was those types of things. They have always had those little interruptions because they were like family. He spent more time with these guys growing up than he did with his own family.

Because of everyone's solo success they had become somewhat divos. They were all making individual requests. Bobby wanted to stay at one hotel while everyone else wanted to stay at another. It wasn't like they were rolling like a group. Everyone demanded their own space. They had separate tour buses with their own separate entourages. Everyone had their own separate demands as to what they wanted. The tour became what it was, different solo acts touring as a group.

The one thing that was missing on this tour that had always been a staple in their old New Edition tours was the groupie fanfare. Although the groupies were there, they weren't allowed access like they were in their earlier years, the reason being most of them had families or just weren't into having a lot of girls anymore. As for Bobby, Whitney made it her business to be at as many shows as possible. She was almost a permanent fixture on the tour. He didn't get a lot of playtime.

Bobby was always considered to be the troublemaker on the tour because of his tardiness and rebellious nature. These attributes always kept him at war with the guys. He missed a few shows and didn't show up for the American Music Awards. Things like this would always get the guys bent out of shape. They would say things like, "I'm just going to be like Bobby and not do it." Or, "Bobby didn't have to do it, so why should I?" Bobby eventually admits that he was a little guilty of being a bad influence on the group.

One of his problems is his sleeping habits. He is like a vampire. He is at his best in the wee hours of the morning. He was always known to sleep all day and be up all night. This habit always caused a conflict with the group's schedule. While working on this album and touring, he would always show up late for practices, video shoots, and photo shoots. (Sometimes five or six hours late.) He had grown accustomed to being a solo artist. So coming back for this reunion was definitely a challenge for him. He was used to calling his own shots and creating his own schedule. Having to conform to being in a group again was a task that definitely caused many arguments and fights, especially because he was dealing with five other divos!

At the end of the day, the reunion was very successful because Bobby eventually admits that he didn't get nothing but great feedback from the fans. All Bobby heard was, "You guys look great; we're so glad to see you all back together." The comments were all positive. There were times when it seemed as though the tour was going to fall apart, but it all worked out!

Although the response was great, soon after the reunion album and tour ended, all the controversy and hype just disappeared into thin air. It was like they came and went in the blink of an eye. Everyone dashed back into their own worlds. It would be years before they all performed together on stage again. The last time the guys got together and did something really big was when they stole the show at BET's 25th anniversary in October 2005. The media was saying that it was the biggest thing since the Jacksons stole the show at the Motown anniversary some years ago. Bobby recalls, "It really felt good being back on the stage with all of the guys. I think the crowd really enjoyed it as well. Everybody got out of their seats and danced right along with us."

Don't think that you have seen the last of them. This year is the 20th anniversary of the *Don't Be Cruel* album and the 25th anniversary of the first New Edition album.

They will all be back together touring soon. Although they do spot dates here and there, they have to give the world a real tour. As a matter of fact, Bobby says, "As long as we are all healthy, I think we will tour forever, whenever our schedules permit it."

The difference with Bobby and the guys these days is they are all grown men now. Their relationship is totally different than when they were young guys trying to find themselves. "I realized that these are my friends who are like family that I love dearly," says Bobby. "These are guys that I grew up with, learned life with, became a man with, and I love them all. I think we are all looking forward to going back on tour together. I know it's gonna be a lot of fun. Regardless of what happens or what else we do with our careers, we will always be New Edition!"

Friendly Feuds

The So-Called Usher Fight . . . and More

On one odd night Bobby did something he doesn't normally do with other celebrities. He showed up at Usher's birthday party to congratulate him on his success and wish him a happy birthday. He's not big on going to celebrity functions and doing the whole Hollywood thing. In this case, it was more like going to support a little brother.

When he walked into the party, he ran into a lot of people he hadn't seen in a long time. He hadn't been out partying in a while, so he felt a little uncomfortable. It wasn't long before he made his way to the bar to order a drink. He ordered one of his favorites, vodka on the rocks. Three shots of this and he was ready to take on the world. All guards were down and he was loose and ready to mingle.

About an hour later, Bobby ran into Usher, and they immediately gave each other a hug. "While he was holding me, he turned to the side and kinda put my neck in a playful chokehold and started squeezing me," Bobby explains. "I tried to tell him that I couldn't breathe, but he couldn't hear me because the music was loud. It didn't help that he was drunk. I was yelling, 'Yo, yo, yo, let me go! I can't breathe!' He was excited to see me and he was just expressing himself with this gesture. He was so drunk he didn't realize what he was doing. Usher is a pretty strong guy, so he had a tight hold on my neck. The more I was yelling, 'I'm serious, I can't breathe,' the more he began to laugh saying,

'Yeah, yeah, yeah.' I was a little woozy myself, so all of my thoughts weren't rational as it related to coming up with a solution to convince Usher that he had me in a very twisted position. So out of reflex, I picked him up and held him over the DJ booth, which had a nice little drop down below. When I did this, I guess his bodyguards felt like I was threatening his life, so they came to his rescue. They came and pulled us apart, which looked like a scuffle to the people around looking on. That's how the whole situation got blown out of proportion. The onlookers and media put it out there that Usher and I had a fight at the club when it was only horseplay." He continues, "I mean, I don't show up at people's parties to start trouble. That's not what I'm about. Of course, by the time the media put their twist on it, it was 'Bobby Brown gets in a fight with Usher at his birthday party!' It was totally blown out of proportion."

Showing up at Usher's party was very unusual for him, mainly because he doesn't really deal with a lot of people in the industry. Bobby reveals, "I might hang out or party sometimes, but I never really become friends with them. I've had a couple of people in the industry whom I thought were friends, but our relationships ended up on a sour note. This gave me a bad taste. LA Reid, for example, was a really good friend, but he turned 'corporate' on me, which to me means he started acting like a female dog. First of all, he stole from Whitney, which means he stole from our friendship. Anybody that takes from my family takes from me. When he got his CEO position at Arista Records, he signed Whitney to a major deal, which I backed 100 percent considering we were friends. He ended up taking her album and mishandling it along with some other things. He did poor promotions and didn't support it like we felt he should. In our opinion, he was bootlegging the project. In terms of sales, this was the worst album released in Whitney's career, and it was all because of him. Therefore, our friendship will forever be challenged by this. It's something I can never forgive him for. Or shall I say I can forgive but not forget. Based on the relationship we had prior to this, I felt like my manhood had been tested. So in order to keep the peace, it was best for him to go his way and me to go mine."

Early in his career, LA Reid and Babyface were producers on his biggest album, so he always respected them. They had some great times. They celebrated the success of his *Don't Be Cruel* album together. There's nothing like being a part of a project with a group of people and watching the project go through the stratosphere. There are a lot of emotions shared and much champagne toasting! Although they enjoyed being on top of the world together at one point, he is no longer in communication with either of them. He fell out with Babyface years ago because they couldn't get along, and recently he and L.A. have severed their ties.

At this time in his life, his friendships in the industry were very limited, and he doesn't have a problem with keeping it that way. The industry is filled with a bunch of fakeness that he can live without. He's going to let them do what they do, and he's going to keep on being Bobby!

Chapter 9

Being Bobby Brown

"The Press, More Problems and Passion for Drugs"

The Twelve-Step Program

Working It Out

" My name is Bobby Brown and I'm an addict."
These are the opening words of every drug
rehab meeting. Bobby's been through the drill so many
times during his two stays at the drug program, it rings
in his head if he even thinks about doing a drug. The
lessons of the drug program are so repetitive that they
will jar your brain. I guess that's the nature of the
program, considering that the mind is a creature of
habit and it responds to repetition. Rehab is cool the
first month, but going into the second month you
become so annoyed it almost makes you want to
relapse.

Bobby's been to the drug program twice. He
believes the first time he went saved his life. "At one
point in my life I was using drugs uncontrollably," he
admits. "I was using everything I could get my hands
on, from cocaine to heroin, weed, and cooked cocaine. I

used to roll the cooked cocaine and weed up into a joint. This was called a laced joint, which was one of my favorites. It always gave me the blast I was looking for."

In those days, getting high was just another part of his day. It was like eating. He had to have it in order to go on. It was like being Pookie from the movie *New Jack City*. Pookie would always say, "Man, I wanna get off these drugs, but they keep callin' me, callin' me."Bobby can joke about this now, but back then it wasn't a laughing matter.

Drugs have the tendency to control you. You have no control over your actions or behavior. The desire takes over, and you become like a zombie walking into the night. It's a disease that I wouldn't wish on my worst enemy.

There were nights when Bobby was on heroin and he would be unconscious for hours. He remembers, "I'd just sit in the chair and nod off. I might sit there for hours and nod. All depending on how good the 'boy' was (*boy* was a nickname for heroin), sometimes it would take a whole day for me to regain my consciousness."

On the infamous night in August 2001, the paramedics had to come and rush him to the hospital. "I overdosed on heroin. I had been getting high all day when I hit the floor unconscious and Whitney had to dial 911. I was so high that I died three times before the ambulance even got there. I also had a severe stroke that caused my heart to stop. The paramedics had to hook up heart paddles to revive me before rushing me off in the ambulance. I stayed in the hospital for weeks after that," he recalls. When he pulled through, he decided he would never use the boy again. This incident left his mouth crooked, and every time he talks his lips turn sideways. This condition came from the stroke he suffered from the overdose. He went to therapy for months in order to regain control of the nerves that caused his lips to malfunction.

Although he never used the boy again, he did continue to use the "girl" (nickname for cocaine). The girl had always been good to him. She never put him under the strains that the boy did. The girl kept him up, whereas the boy made him nod off. The girl kept him on his p's and q's, whereas the boy had him slippin'. The girl just always kept him going. When it came to the girl, he thought he was Scarface. "I had a desk like Scarface in my room," says Bobby, "and I kept the girl piled up on it. Every time I walked past my desk, I'd make a line of coke from one end to the other. I'd take a straw and snort a line the same way Scarface did it in the movie. You couldn't tell me nothing. I felt like I was Tony Montana! The World was Mine! I never had to look for coke; I kept it plentiful. There were times when I went on my binges and would lock myself up in a room for days at a time just getting high." At this point, getting high had become his favorite pastime. There was nothing else in the world that he'd rather be doing. It took him away from the reality of his pain or whatever he was going through at the time. It was an escape from it all. Especially the pressures caused by the price of fame and that which comes with it!

Bobby has sold drugs before, so he always knew the effect they could have on you. Looking back, there were always certain incidents in his life that propelled his drug use. He reflects, "Watching my sister's fiancé get killed definitely caused my drug use to escalate. I can recall that I started drinking heavily when Janet Jackson and I broke up. Before I met Janet, I would never drink hard liquor, I only drank beer. But after our break up, I started drinking hard liquor excessively. I took the way our relationship ended very hard. Not to say we were head-over-heels in love, but she was someone I had a lot of feelings for."

He continues, "I never used cocaine until after I met Whitney. Before then, I had experimented with other drugs, but marijuana was my drug of choice. I had been smoking weed since my New Edition days. This was always a conflict because we were a group that had a clean image. It was kind of hard singing "Popcorn Love" and doing "Just Say No" drug campaigns when I knew I was just as guilty as anybody using. I would have to get on TV and lie to the world. I was not being true to myself."

His desire and passion for drugs has haunted him throughout his life. It started off as one big party and ended up as a dependency. Drugs are definitely nothing to play with. His fight to get off of drugs has been an uphill battle that he feels he will totally overcome, just like everything else he's faced in his life.

Need for Speed

Driving Under the Influence

Bobby is somewhat of an adrenaline junkie. He has a heavy foot that seems to always get him in trouble. Every time he bought an expensive sports car, he had to test it out.

A lot of his arrests came from speeding cases. He would get pulled over for speeding and catch two or three more charges. On one occasion, he was pulled over for speeding in Atlanta. When the officer ran his name he found out that he had a warrant for failing to appear on other traffic charges. When he searched the truck he found marijuana. So now Bobby received a marijuana charge. He didn't have his license, so the officer charged him with that. This is how it usually went. It would start off with him speeding, and he would end up being locked up ten times for different things under that speeding violation. The multiple charges made things seem like they were a lot worse than they actually were.

In 1996, once again his need for speed got him in trouble. This time it turned out tragically. He broke four ribs and his foot when he lost control of Whitney's Porsche. "This was another time I saw my life flash before me," says Bobby. "I hopped in the car and started speeding down the highway and all of a sudden the brakes went out on the car. I was going around a curve when the car spun out of control, jumped the curb, and hit a street sign. At that moment, it seemed like a scene in a movie. Everything was in slow motion.

I watched myself in the car going through the motions. I thought my life was over." When the police and medics arrived, they rushed him to the hospital, where his blood was checked for alcohol and drugs. When the tests came back four months later, they said that his blood alcohol level was twice the limit, which he felt was the furthest thing from the truth. It seemed really strange that it took four months to get the results back. When he went to trial on those charges, he lost the case, and the judge made an example out of him. He sentenced him to five days in jail, thirty days at a drug rehab, 100 hours of community service, and a $500 fine.

To make matters worse, although he wasn't drunk at the time of the wreck, on the day he showed up to start serving his sentence on those charges he had been smoking marijuana and drinking. It wasn't like he was doing this intentionally to aggravate the system. He figured why not be high going to a place that he didn't want to be. Once again, his way of thinking *or not thinking* got him in more trouble. His probation officer reported this to the judge, and the judge added more time to his sentence. A year later another warrant was issued for his arrest on this same charge for a violation of probation. He had tested positive for cocaine at one of his probation visits. He kept getting into different trouble under this same charge, and it all started from a speeding violation. Bobby adds, "I was getting so high during this time that I thanked the judge and told him he saved my life for sending me to rehab." Back then, he had no respect for the law. He was definitely in his rebellious stage, and he figured if he did it, it was his prerogative. The judge knew this, too, because he accused him of "thumbing his nose" at the system.

Bobby learned about the probation system during his experiences of being repeatedly arrested for the same charge. "I think probation is just a get-out-of-jail-free card until you get into something else," says Bobby. "Then they can put you in jail and throw away the key. It could be something as simple as jaywalking. The only way you can avoid violating probation is to lock yourself up in a house and become a nun." It got to the point where he would choose thirty days in jail instead of one year of probation if the judge gave him the option when he went to court. "I took the thirty days in jail because I knew that if I took the probation and so much as sneezed too hard I'd be in jail anyway, and the probation would start all over again when I got out," he recalls. Instead of taking that chance, he'd take the thirty days, so that when he got out he would be done with the charge altogether. It took him being arrested several times to finally figure this out.

I Fought the Law

The Law Won

It seemed like at one stage of his life trouble became his shadow. It followed him wherever he went. Everywhere he went there was drama. It's not like he was looking for it; it just seemed to find him.

"First of all, I'm a family man. Everybody knows that in order to run a household you have to have some kind of responsibility. A responsible person doesn't go out starting things with people like a bully or gang member or something. The way I've been portrayed in the media is like I was a guy that had nothing else to do with my time but create problems," says Bobby. For instance, he was at a night club in Orlando, Florida, at Disney World with some friends back in 1995. A drunk man started acting belligerent and obnoxious. They tried to calm him down, but he insisted on being rude and disrespectful. "Before I knew it, he spit on him. I believe that's the filthiest thing you can do to a man," says Bobby. "My friends and I beat him to a pulp. We made sure he wouldn't spit on nobody else. By the time we got through with him, one whole side of his face was ripped up, and a part of his ear was on the ground. We all ended up going to jail that night, and I had to pay $30,000 to get us out of that mess."

"Ever since I was a kid, I was taught to protect myself and my family. If someone disrespects me or my family, they are gonna hear from me. I'm not disrespectful to anyone, and I'm not going to be disrespected by anyone. My father always taught me, 'If someone hits you, then hit them back harder.' That has always stuck with me," reveals Bobby.

He continues, "This man who blatantly disrespected me wouldn't have been laid up in the hospital with his ear torn off trying to sue me if he hadn't approached me in that way. That goes for anyone. They step to me wrong, and I whoop that tail; then they want to sue." I guess that's the nature of being a celebrity. You are an automatic target for certain people and their foolishness. His philosophy has always been, "you deal with me as a man, and I will deal with you as such."

This man ended up suing Bobby, and he settled out of court to keep from going through the hassle. He always pleaded guilty or settled if he knew he was wrong. But if he felt he was right, he was going to trial.

Going back and forth in the system, he learned a lot. If he felt he was right about a case, he would always go to trial and fight the charges. For instance, he went to trial for the drunken driving case where he drove the Porsche off the road. They were saying that his blood-alcohol level was twice the limit, when he knew he hadn't been drinking that day. He might've been drinking on a whole lot of other occasions, but he wasn't drunk on this day. He admits that he was speeding but he was not drunk. Do you know how it feels to know you're innocent but get railroaded because of your past behavior or your capability of doing something of that nature? This is how he felt. It's a mixed feeling of complete deceit, defeat, and frustration. The thing that was so peculiar about this case was that the police waited four months to charge him. It supposedly took them four months to run tests on his blood so they could charge him with drunken driving. During the trial, his attorneys attacked the handling of blood evidence and the motives of the police to wait four months to charge him. They felt like it was definitely a conspiracy. His attorneys felt like the police were targeting his celebrity and his past record. At the end of the day, the jury voted in the police's favor; they came back with a guilty verdict, and Bobby was sentenced harshly.

From this day on, he knew that our justice system was not always completely fair. If they really want to bring you down, they will do anything in their power to do it. Even if that means tampering with evidence. When it gets like that, all you can do is throw your hands up and say, "You win!"

Chapter 10

Coming to His Senses

"Bobby's Wake-up Call"

Dealing with Divorce

Don't Believe the Hype

66 I feel like my marriage to Whitney was doomed from the very beginning," says Bobby. Within the first year they separated, with several reconciliations and more separations to follow. Bobby explains, "I think we got married for all the wrong reasons. Now I realize Whitney had a different agenda than I did when we got married. Although I felt we had great chemistry and were best friends as well as lovers, getting married was a huge step. I believe her agenda was to clean up her image, while mine was to be loved and have children." At that time, Whitney was under a lot of pressure. The media was accusing her of having a bisexual relationship with her assistant, Robin Crawford. Since she was the American Sweetheart and all, that didn't go to well with her image. This topic was no secret; you could pick up any magazine or tabloid in the world, and there would be information about Whitney's sexual desire for women.

Everyone in the music industry knows that image is everything. So when these types of things happen to the talent making the big money, people at the top start to panic. They don't need anything like this interfering with their money. Therefore, everyone in public relations tries to come up with solutions to solve the problem. The big bosses' main concern is to get rid of the problem. Whatever it takes.

In Whitney's situation, the only solution was to get married and have kids. That would kill all speculation, whether it was true or not. Bobby got caught up in the politics and ended up marrying one of the biggest stars in the world. The top-level executives didn't think it was going to last as long as it did. They probably didn't think they were going to fall in love the way they did. Once they found out how they truly felt and how strong their connection was, they started trying to break them up and NEVER stopped!

Everyone expected Whitney to do what Diana Ross (America's other black pop princess) did and marry a white man. So when she married Bobby, everyone was shocked. You had some critics saying that they wouldn't be together for a year. Then two years rolled by. Then they started saying they wouldn't make it for five years. Then once five years rolled around they stopped making predictions. They made a believer out of everybody. They ended up going almost fifteen years strong. The whole time they were together, the only thing critics could do was concentrate on the negative side of their relationship. They started turning up the heat with giving them bad press. Any dirt they could find, true or not, they slang it!

"I feel like several people wanted to see us divorced," says Bobby. "So they took part in coming between us. Everybody had their own opinions as to what they thought should happen between us. It's kind of hard being in a relationship when you have other people—friends, family, and business associates—constantly in your ear. Whitney and I would have to disassociate ourselves from everyone for periods at a time just to maintain our sanity."

He continues, "On one hand, we had Whitney's parents, especially her dad, telling her, "He's no good for you. You have to get rid of him before he destroys you." On the other hand, we had her business associates, or people trying to make money off of her, telling her, "I know you could straighten out if you didn't have that man around." As if that wasn't enough to deal with, she also had a half-brother, in-laws, and scandalous sister-in-laws trying to start controversy about her only to blackmail her and keep their hands in her pockets."

"Let's not forget about or rule out my family. My own sister was running to the tabloids selling stories, which didn't make things any better. There were a whole lot of things happening around us that made it impossible for us to go on."

Although others played a part in his divorce, Bobby won't neglect to admit his faults. "I know that I definitely contributed to our marital problems," he admits. "I am guilty of sleeping with other women as well as other offenses." I'm sure you have heard all the stories by now. The cover of every tabloid magazine ran things like "Bobby seen coming out of hotel with younger woman" or "Bobby to father child outside of marriage." Some of these headlines were true, but most were totally made up. "I must admit, it's hard being a man in my position and married," says Bobby. "Women are always throwing themselves at you. I'm only human, so I would make the mistake and bite the hook sometimes. The fact that I was using drugs didn't help my decision-making process. It wasn't that I didn't love my wife or that it was something she wasn't doing; I was only being a man. I let the testosterone take over. Most successful men are guilty of this. I was just the one always getting caught. You live, you learn."

One story in particular that made headline news was a rumor that he was leaving Whitney to be with Karrine "Supahead" Steffans. They were also saying that they were planning to get married. This was the furthest thing from the truth. What people didn't know is that Whitney and Bobby had not been together for two years prior to their divorce proceedings. During this time, he developed a relationship with Karrine, but he had no intentions of making her his woman. He explains, "Karrine was a chick who had built her name by giving oral pleasure and sleeping around with half the entertainment industry, including other women's husbands. Then she had the audacity to write a book degrading these men, myself included. That's how she got the nickname "Supahead." I mean, come on, I deserve more credit than that. What do I look like being married to one of the best things that happened to the industry, to drop all the way down and marry one of the worst things that happened to the industry, a woman who made a career of kissing and telling! I don't care what the media has made you think about my state of mind or how many drugs I have used, all I have to say is, 'My marbles aren't that loose!'"

"Yes, she was a friend of mine," he continues. "Yes, I've slept with her. Yes, I've spent several nights at her house. But she was only good for what her nickname stood for and nothing else. Not to mention the fact that she is a terrible mother to her kids. If there is one thing I can't stand, that's a woman who is not a mother to her children. That's a big turnoff to me!"

"The bottom line is, Karrine is out to make a quick buck at the expense of others. I also think she needs some psychological help. She has been mentally and emotionally scarred throughout her life. She definitely needs a hug!"

His highly publicized relationship with Karrine was the last incident that happened before he and Whitney were officially separated in September 2006. He feels like the Karrine situation was just a public excuse for Whitney to divorce him, but as he just mentioned, technically they had been unofficially split up for about two years prior to that. It was like they didn't live together; they didn't even talk that much. He was living at home with their daughter while Whitney spent most of her nights sleeping over her friend Cherelle's house. She'd leave home and be gone for weeks at a time doing whatever she wanted. Bobby had grown tired of her shenanigans, so he started living his life as a single man.

Whitney filed for divorce in October, one month after their official separation. Her reason in the petition was irreconcilable differences, and the differences that were listed were old news. She claimed things like drug addiction, alleged infidelity, an arrest on suspicion of domestic abuse, and trial separation—pretty much things they had already been through. That's why he knew the reason she wanted a divorce had something to do with the influence of other people.

Seven months later, in April 2007, their divorce was finalized. However, he was not happy with some of the stipulations, so Bobby filed a lawsuit against Whitney and her attorneys in an attempt to change them. The first was the terms of custody for their daughter. Whitney was granted full custody of Bobbi Kris because he didn't make a court-appointed deadline. He didn't make it because Whitney told him not to worry about the petition. She constantly reassured him that she would have her lawyers back off. She told him he had at least six months to deal with it, and then she turned around and sped the process up, knowing that he wasn't financially and emotionally ready to deal with this. With all that was going on, he had become very depressed. "I thought she would be sympathetic about my condition, but evidently she wasn't," recalls Bobby. The court eventually took away his rights altogether to see his daughter, which infuriated him. He didn't feel like this was fair.

In addition to suing for custody of his daughter, he also sued for spousal support since he sacrificed a lot of his personal life and gave up his career to help Whitney with hers. "Whitney had persuaded me to take a break from working," says Bobby. "She would say things like, 'I only have a couple of more years in the industry. You're younger than me, so you can take off for another five years, and by the time my career is up, you'll be ready to go again.' At the time, this sounded really good, and I couldn't see any reason why it wouldn't work. But when that time finally came for me to restart my career, I got served divorce papers." Granting her wishes of taking a break and putting his career on hold definitely hindered his personal financial stability and left him in a difficult position. Therefore, due to lack of funds during the divorce, his living arrangements and other things were compromised. He was forced to stay with friends and family, among other things, during this trying time in his life.

When he and Whitney got married they had a prenuptial agreement that stated all of their property was separate. So basically they would walk away with whatever they came with. Of course, that would have worked in her favor because she had the most. However, in court she never presented a copy of the document, nor did he, so he was able to follow through with the spousal support lawsuit.

"I feel sorry for the things that happened between us," says Bobby. "I think one day we'll sit down and talk about everything, and she'll finally understand." Since he regained the rights of visitation with his daughter, he and Whitney still see each other from time to time. They are co-parents to their child. They go out to restaurants and discuss things that need to be resolved. Although they have a few issues to settle in court, "they are still friends. "Whitney always was and always will be my buddy," says Bobby.

Sobering Up

The Process

Bobby's wake-up call literally came one night from his two daughters. He had been on one of his binges when Bobbi Kris and La Princia got together and telephoned him. He remembers this conversation as if it was yesterday. "They said, 'Dad, we've had enough, we're gonna kill you if you hurt yourself. You mean too much to us to see you go through this.' Two of my kids confronting me with my destructive behavior was like a dagger in the heart. My life changed at that moment. The person that came up with the phrase 'Words can cut like a knife if they come from the right person' was so right! My daughters mean everything to me, so to have them call me and pour their hearts out was very emotional and life changing."

As a result, he's sober now. He's been sober for almost a year. Sobering up is a strenuous process that is ongoing. Sober for him means he's gotten off the hard drugs, but he still drinks his brew. Everyone that knows him knows he loves Budweiser. He drinks it throughout the day. Just like most people wake up and have their morning cup of coffee, he wakes up to a cold can of Budweiser. He's been drinking beer so long that he thinks his body is becoming immune to it. It takes a lot to affect him.

Another bad habit he really wants to kick is smoking cigarettes. "This is the hardest one," says Bobby. "I really like smoking because it keeps me calm and keeps my hands occupied. It doesn't help that I've been smoking since I was a kid. Old habits are the hardest habits to break."

He does a lot of working out right now. He watches what he eats also. He tries to eat as healthy as possible. He thinks working out is definitely a great part of the sobering up process. It does a lot with repairing the body that has been broken down by drug abuse. It also helps him build his wind up for stage performances, although no matter what condition his body is in, whenever he hits the stage, "I get an adrenaline rush that sends my body into autopilot," reveals Bobby. "I might sweat a lot, but I always perform at top level."

Throughout his career he always made it a point not to drink or get high before he went on stage. He always needed to be clearheaded before he went on. He didn't indulge in any of these activities until after he came off the stage. Then it was like a celebration after a championship game. I'll toast to that!

Life for him is different now; it is not so much about celebrating as it is about having peace of mind. Being off of hard drugs definitely brings much more clarity and order to his life. Unlike the past, life is more about substance now as opposed to partying. Everything has meaning. It's all about morals and values. He feels like he's finally come to his senses.

At Peace with Thyself

Facing the Man in the Mirror

Being sober has given Bobby a second wind. His days are clearer now. "I feel like performing again, making records again, on a major level!" says Bobby. "I feel like the old Bobby." The old Bobby is very hard on himself when it comes to making music. "I'm a perfectionist," says Bobby. "When I'm in the studio I like to run a song down. I will do it over and over again until I feel it's right. That's the space that I am in now. I want to resurrect a career that will leave a mark on the world like I had in the past." He continues, "That's why I practice constantly. My comeback has to have an impact. I feel like even when you're practicing, you are supposed to give it your all, just like you do when you're on stage. I try to have that same energy when I'm rehearsing that I have during a live show, so that it's for real. When you do this, you learn something new about your performance every time."

He realizes that he's getting up in age and this might be his last time around, so he's going to give it his all. One thing he learned about the music business is that you have to take it one step at a time because you never know what's gonna happen. Therefore, he's open to exploring new ideas and trying new experiences at this point in his life.

He just finished a reality show called *Goin' Country*, hosted by John Rich, of the country duo Big & Rich. He competed with several other music stars from different genres of music: Carnie Wilson, formerly of

Wilson Phillips; Dee Snider of Twisted Sister; American Idol finalist, Diana DeGarmo; Julio Iglesias, Jr.; Maureen McCormick ("The Brady Bunch"); and R&B artist Sisqo. They competed for a chance to win a contract to record a country music album. This show was very therapeutic for him.

Filming this reality show caused him to be more vulnerable than he has ever been in public—even more vulnerable than he was on his reality show, *Being Bobby Brown*. Throughout the show, he shed a few tears. First of all, country music is a form of music that is written about different issues that we friend's pick-up truck in my girlfriend's driveway," or "she broke my achy breaky heart." The song he came up with was a country ballad called "The Man," which is a very emotional and personal piece that covers things he's been through in his life, from being locked up to other issues. Performing this song really broke him down. Another time that really touched his heart was visiting the hospital where there were children suffering from cancer.

The weirdest thing he had to deal with was admitting to the world that he has a sleeping disorder. While sleep walking, the cameras caught him using the restroom in some very unusual places. This was pretty wild.

Gaining approval in the country world was a more serious experience than he expected. Writing his country song caused him to face some unresolved issues in his life. Although he didn't win, the overall experience was definitely life changing.

Each day, he is learning to put his trust more in God. He asks for His guidance every step of the way. As you have seen throughout his life, he is guilty of succumbing to the temptations that almost every human being faces. That's human nature. Our Creator created us that way. It's how we as people handle and overcome the challenges that we encounter that determines our destiny. Every man's journey is different.

He has accepted and overcome his challenges as they presented themselves. One thing that he has learned is that they will continue to present themselves. "Even though I walk through the Valley of the shadow of death, I will fear no evil, for you are with me; your rod and your staff, they comfort me" (Psalm 23). This scripture has always resonated in his heart and given him strength when he needed it.

Bobby's aware of the fact that Whitney has been seeing Ray J, a very young R&B artist who is most famous for being the little brother of Brandy, the multiplatinum singing artist and TV star. "Their relationship doesn't bother me," says Bobby. "She's open to see whoever she wants to see, just like I can see who I want to see. I know the age difference between her and the little guy is about twenty years, but it's to each his own. The only concern I had was how our daughter felt about the age difference. As long as she's cool with it, then it's fine with me."

He's at a place now in his life where he doesn't let things bother him. He's endured pretty much any and everything personally and publicly, so at this point, he doesn't sweat the small stuff. He just lets things roll off his back. However, one of the things that he does value is his space. He needs space and time to get himself together and gather his thoughts. He has a young lady in his life by the name of Alicia Etheridge who helps him keep it all together. He has known Alicia for over sixteen years. They've always been good friends. She is an executive in the music industry and has been behind the scenes assisting and managing many artists' careers. Recently she committed to helping him get his career back on track. They have established a special relationship that blends the business and pleasure. Right now they are really close friends, but who knows what the future holds.

It has been rumored that Alicia was a friend of Whitney's that is backstabbing her because of her relationship with Bobby. The truth is she has never met Whitney in her life. She has spoken to her briefly on the phone once through a mutual friend while they were going through their divorce. So I guess you can say they know of each other, but they are definitely not friends.

Bobby knows half the people expected him to use this book to trash his ex-wife. Well, no! He's not that low! But what I can tell you is that, yes, maybe some of the things you have heard or read about her have some truth to them, and I will neither confirm it nor deny them. What Bobby has done is given you the truth, the whole truth, and nothing but the truth by admitting all of his faults and the things he's done. If his ex-wife ever wants to write a book on her life in the future, then he'll let her tell you her story! Whitney is someone that he loves dearly as a person and the mother of his child. They have been through a lot together and have grown a lot together through all of their trials and tribulations, so all he can say is she will always have a place in his heart!

Bobby's at a point in his life where it's more about surrounding himself with supportive people and establishing good and trusting friendships. He's realized the importance of having people around you that have your best interest at heart, so he concentrates on that aspect of a relationship.

Currently, he is at peace with himself, and he would just like for his family and friends to be happy. "More than anything, I want my kids to be healthy and to feel loved," says Bobby. That's why I go out of my way to have relationships with their mothers, regardless of what we go through."

Who knows how the Bobby Brown story is going to end. Will he end up back at the altar or where is his career going to take him? He might end up in Vegas headlining Caesars Palace, or maybe he'll end up on the old-school tour circuit headlining with the groups of his prime-time era. Who knows? Only time will tell.

"One thing I do know is if I had a chance to live my life all over again, I wouldn't change a thing," says Bobby. I think we all have to go through life lessons and learn how to grow from our mistakes. Mistakes Bobby has definitely made! It's nothing that he's ashamed of or that he hasn't grown from. He's still learning and growing. That's a process that I believe is never ending!

Ronnie and I playing Tug of War. We were about 13 years old.

Me with my nieces and nephews at Easter in Boston: Me, MeMe, Jairam, Kelsey, Hakim, Sharee, Tiny, and Shane.

Ralph blessing a fan with one of our New Edition plaques.

New Edition's first tour jacket.

Ronnie and Michael getting ready for a dance competition.

Me chillin' on the top of a car around the age of 16.

Me on the mic during my rap solo in concert.

Me allowing my nephew Kelsey to get a taste of stardom at my concert.

Me at rehearsal for my performance on The Arsenio Hall Show.

Nate Smith, LA Reid, me, Tommy (my brother and manager), and Babyface.

Me as a guest on The Oprah Winfrey Show. *Check out my Gumby!*

Me chillin' with Billy at my aunt's house in Boston

Nate, me, and Girky (my bodyguard) eating at a restaurant.

Girky, me, and AJ (my bodyguards) on a shopping spree.

Me and the heavyweight champion, Thomas "Hitman" Hearns and friends.

Me holding my nephew, McKinley Brown.

Tim, Billy, AJ, Dennis, Tony, Nate, me, Girky, and Travis enjoying a meal at Benihana.

Me and a friend on a movie set.

Me and Whitney in the beginning when we were getting to know each other.

Me and Whitney during our happier days.

131

My different look, from the Gumby to bald.

Me, Carolyn Brown (of background dancers, Mecca), Willie, and Derek.

Me clowning before a show with Willie in the background.

Tommy, Pops, Lee Lee, and Coupe (my sisters) at the airport.

Stevie Wonder, Whitney, BeBe and CeCe Winans, and I share a laugh at the Grammy Awards.

Whitney, Freddie Jackson, CeCe Winans, and I pose for the cameras at the Grammy Awards.

Freddie Jackson, me, and BeBe Winans pose for the ladies at the Grammy Awards.

Me giving the crowd what they want on my Don't Be Cruel Tour.

Me being taken to jail for non-payment of child support to Kim.

Me flying through the crowd on my high-tech Don't Be Cruel Tour.

Me with both of my background dancers, Heart & Soul (Derek and Willie), and Mecca (Caroly, Merylin, Shane, and Saleema).

Me and Heart & Soul.

Me turning the crowd out on the Don't Be Cruel Tour.

Ma enjoying the moment at my 30th birthday party.

Me and Whitney enjoying a private vacation on the exclusive St. Barth Island.

A snapshot from my wedding.

Me showing Whitney that I'm a strong man!

Me performing at the Phillps Arena in Atlanta, Georgia.

My tour jacket sold on the Don't Be Cruel Tour.

Girky, me, and AJ arriving backstage at my concert.

Girky and me on one of my shopping sprees.

Me and friends being recognized at a private club.

Me and Tommy pose for fans at a private club.

Me and Princess Hamida (the niece of the Sultan of Brunei).

AJ, a friend, Pops, and Lee Lee in Brunei resting before my performance for the Sultan of Brunei's niece, Princess Hamida.

Trina Broussard (my background singer) and I hangin' in Brunei.

Me doing a goofy impersonation of my man Martin Lawrence.

Me on a family vacation enjoying a private moment.

Bobbi Kris (my daughter with Whitney) and my niece Blaire enjoying a boat ride on our family vacation.

Whitney, Carolyn, and me posing for fans as we dine out.

Tina (my sister) and Tommy sharing a laugh at a family dinner.

Me, Whitney, Lee Lee, Pops, Coupe, Tommy, and Carolyn pose at Whitney's birthday celebration.

R&B artist Ciara, the lady in red, Kim Porter, me, Carolyn, Eboni Elektra, Coupe, and Philana Williams at a private house party.

Tina, Tommy and Carolyn (my sister-n-law at the time), Coupe, LeLe, Bethy (my sisters), Whitney, and me.

Me about to board a private jet.

Me in deep thought on the private jet on the way to my show.

The pilot, Tommy, and me aboard a private jet on the way to my show.

Me showing off my 6-pack, performing at a private club.

Me pleasing the ladies on the mic.

Merylin, Shane, Carolyn, and me enjoying a night out on the town in Las Vegas.

Anybody remember Laverne?

Mike Dobson and me showing off our tattoos.

Me, Whitney, and Bobbi Kris shopping at Universal Studios' City Walk.

Me and Whitney greeting the natives on our spiritual journey to Jerusalem.

Pops, Whitney, Tommy, Lil Bobby, LaPrincia, me, and Bobby Kris posing for my reality TV show, Being Bobby Brown.

Landon, my oldest son.

Me and Whitney on our Jerusalem trip.

Whitney and I dressed for the MTV Video Awards.

Me playing tour guide on a tour bus.

Kim Tillery, Coupe, Desiree, and I chillin'.

My brother's wedding party: Lil Derek, Hakim, Ernest, Ron, KB, me, Tommy, Kenny, Nate, Billy, Novie and Shane.

The entire Brown clan at Tommy's wedding: Dale, Carole, Me, Lee Lee, Pops, Ma, Carolyn, Tommy, Bethy, Tina, Kenny, Carlita, Hakim, Antoine, Anthony, Meta, Shan, Kanita, Shawn, Robert, and Sharee.

Me, Tommy, and BeBe Winans at the wedding.

Me being the best man I could be at his wedding.

A fan created this picture.

Me and Derrick Handspike hangin' out at one of the hot spots in the ATL.

Alicia and I posing before my concert in Atlanta.

Alicia keeping me company while I get a cut before my concert.

149

Alicia patiently waiting on me to get ready for my concert.

Stylz and I clowning in the ATL.

Made in United States
Orlando, FL
03 September 2022

21912443R00091